YULETIDE JAZZ

— PIANO LEVEL —
LATE INTERMEDIATE/EARLY ADVANCED

To access audio, visit:
www.halleonard.com/mylibrary

Enter Code
4612-7846-5118-4741

ISBN 978-1-4234-8263-5

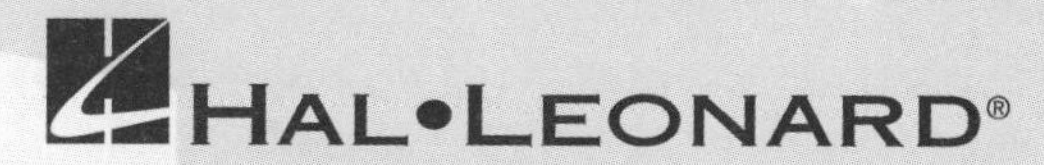

Visit Hal Leonard Online at
www.halleonard.com

Visit Phillip at
www.phillipkeveren.com

Contact us:
Hal Leonard
7777 West Bluemound Road
Milwaukee, WI 53213
Email: info@halleonard.com

In Europe, contact:
Hal Leonard Europe Limited
42 Wigmore Street
Marylebone, London, W1U 2RN
Email: info@halleonardeurope.com

In Australia, contact:
Hal Leonard Australia Pty. Ltd.
4 Lentara Court
Cheltenham, Victoria, 3192 Australia
Email: info@halleonard.com.au

PREFACE

Like holly and ivy, silver and gold, and Currier & Ives, Christmas and jazz just seem to go together well. After more than half a century, Nat King Cole's jazz-tinged ode to roasting chestnuts is still one of our most popular holiday songs. I personally cannot imagine December without Vince Guaraldi's jazz piano and the Peanuts gang.

So, it should not come as a great surprise that I thoroughly loved arranging this collection! I hope you will enjoy these settings as you celebrate the season with family and friends.

A word or two about the recording… I stepped into the studio on a warmish day in May, which seems to be par for the course when it comes to preparing Christmas music for publication. I was aiming for complete performances that maintained the spirit of the arrangements, and did not want to edit snippets together into a whole. Therefore, I allowed small details that do not match the score to make it onto the recordings. That's jazz, folks! I hope these interpretations will help you to better understand my intentions in the printed music.

Merry Christmas and a Jazzy New Year,
Phillip Keveren

BIOGRAPHY

Phillip Keveren, a multi-talented keyboard artist and composer, has composed original works in a variety of genres from piano solo to symphonic orchestra. Mr. Keveren gives frequent concerts and workshops for teachers and their students in the United States, Canada, Europe, and Asia. Mr. Keveren holds a B.M. in composition from California State University Northridge and an M.M. in composition from the University of Southern California.

CONTENTS

ANGELS WE HAVE HEARD ON HIGH

Traditional French Carol
Arranged by Phillip Keveren

17
Gm7 C7 Fmaj7/C B♭ G(add2)/B C(add2) D♭maj7 C
20
F(add2)/A C(add2)/E F/E♭ B♭/D B♭m/D♭ C7sus C7 Am7♭5 D7♯9(♭13) A♭13♭9
p
f
23
Gm7 C13 G♭9 Fmaj7 B♭/D B♭m/D♭ Csus C7/B♭
26
F/A Gm/B♭ Fmaj7/C B♭m/D♭ D7sus D7 E♭(add2) E♭ G♭maj7 F(add2)
rit. e dim.
p
30
D♭maj7 G♭maj9 E♭m11 C♭9
mp a tempo

34
D♭
B♭m9
G♭maj7
D♭maj9/A♭
E♭m7/A♭
cresc.
f
dim.
38
D♭maj7/A♭
A♭9
D♭/A♭
A♭7
D♭maj7
p
pp
cresc.
42
A♭9
G♭/A♭
B♭m
Adim7
D♭/A♭
G♭
Fsus
F
Gmaj7/A
A7♭9
f
46
Dmaj7
F13
Em7
E6
Am7
A13
Dmaj7
D6
Em7
F♯m7
Gmaj7
A13♭9
B♭13♭9
A13
ff
molto rit.
50
C9
A/B
B♭9♯5
A9
Em9(add4)
E♭13(♯11)
D6/9♯11
8va
p
mf
pp

AWAY IN A MANGER/SILENT NIGHT

Arranged by Phillip Keveren

A♭maj9 Gm9
G♭9
F6/9
B♭maj9
Am9
18
p
E♭maj7(♯4)
A♭13
G13
E♭9♯11
D♭9♯11
B♭/C
C9
23
mf
Tempo I
C pedal
27
p
AWAY IN A MANGER
Music by JAMES R. MURRAY
Tempo II
Fmaj9
Dm9
32
rit.
mp
B♭maj7
Am7
Gm7
Fmaj7
C7
8va
36
p

40
B♭ F Fmaj7 B♭maj7/C
G(add2)
G+ D♭9♯11 C6/9
f
45
G(add2)/B
C(add2)/E
Gmaj7/D
Fmaj7 Em11 E♭
mf
dim. e rit.
SILENT NIGHT
Music by FRANZ X. GRUBER
50
F(add2)
G
F/G
C(add2)
A(add2)
p a tempo
55
E♭ D♭
C
Gmaj7/B
F13♯11
mf
59
B♭9♯5
A9
Fmaj7

63
E♭
E♭/D♭
Cmaj7(add6)
F
Am
G
Fmaj7
mp cresc.
67
E♭(add2)
E♭/D♭
D/C
F13♯11
F7♯9(♭13)
A♭13♯11
F13♯11
f
71
D7♭9(♯11)
B♭13♯11
C/G
F/G
rit.
p
Tempo I
G pedal
75
79
Cmaj7
D/C
molto rit.
mf
pp

UKRAINIAN BELL CAROL

Traditional
Arranged by Phillip Keveren

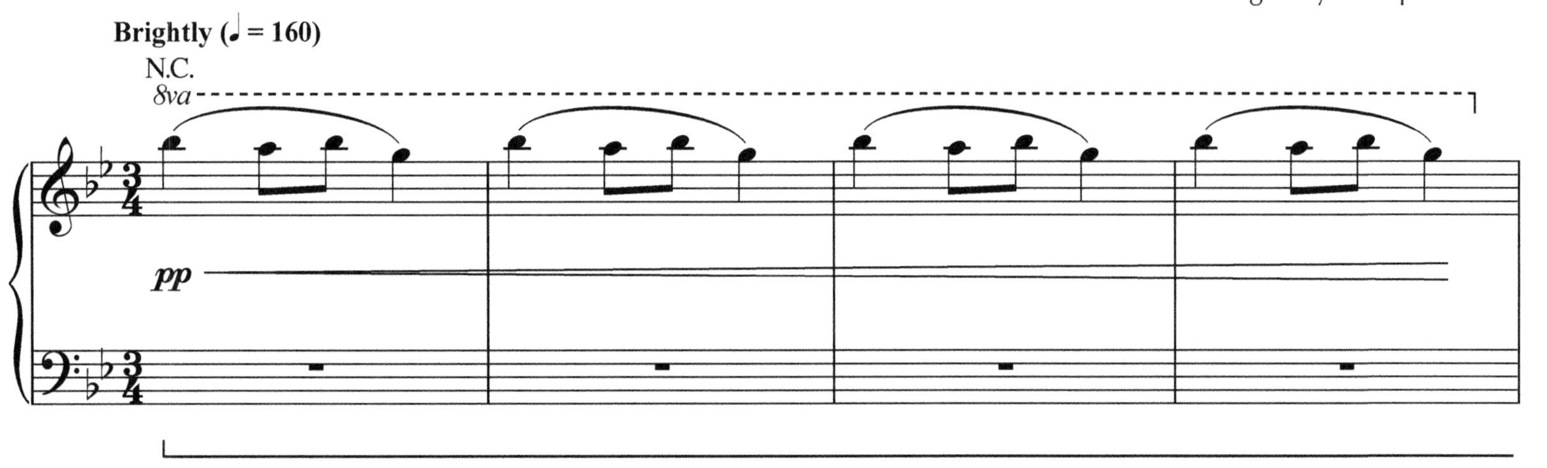

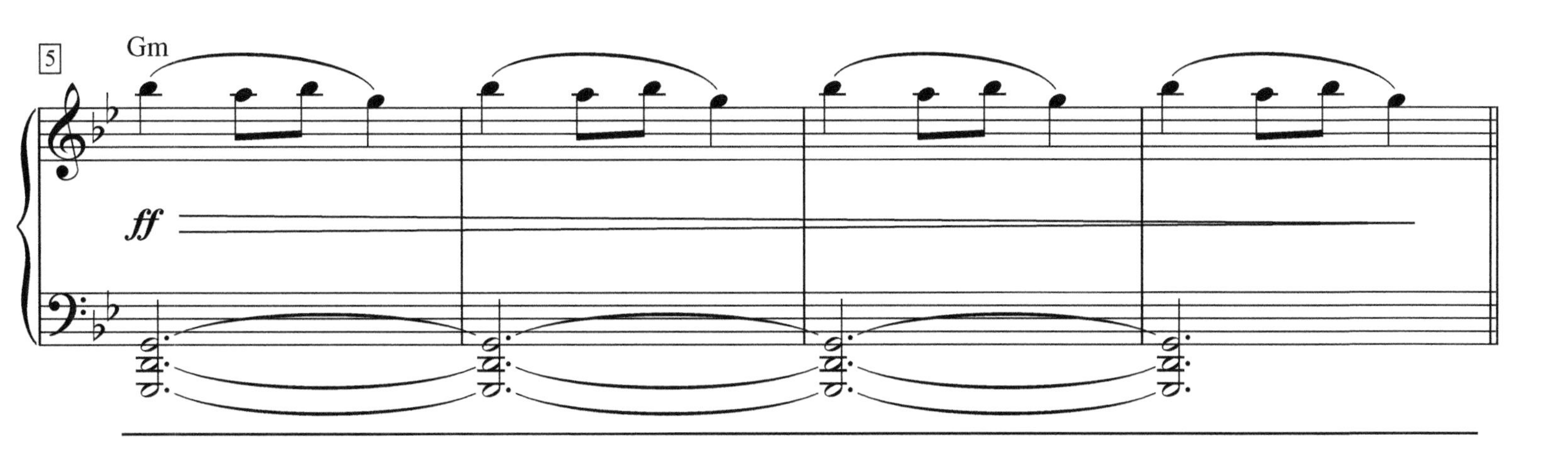

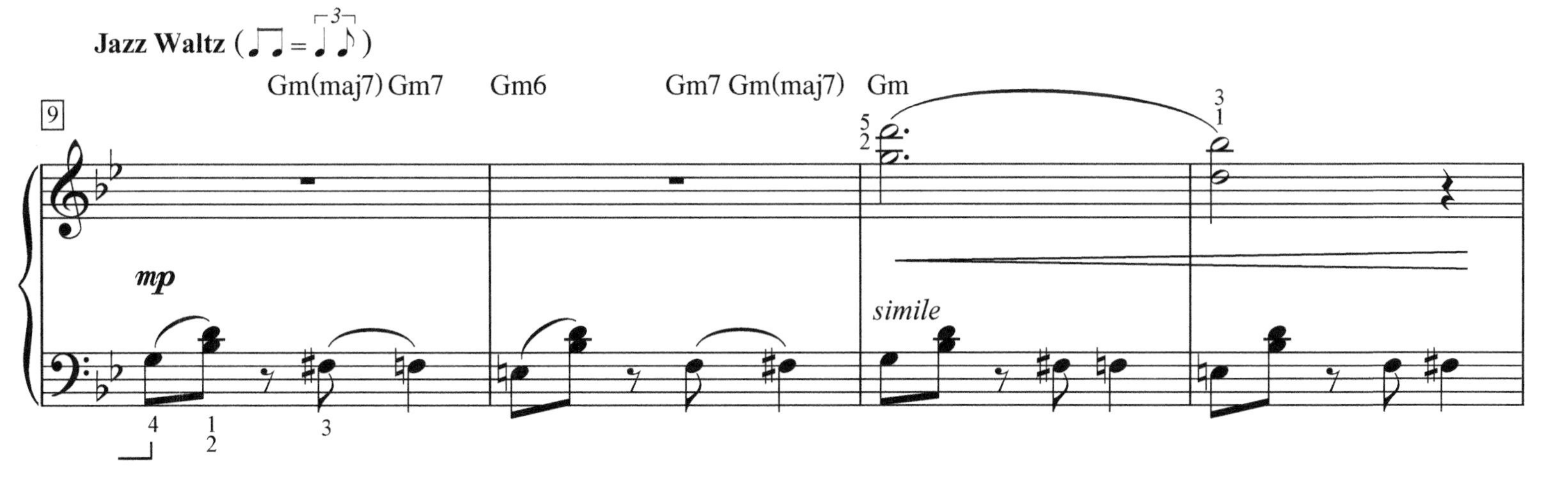

17
Eb/G
Gm
Gdim
Gm
21
Gm(maj7)
Gm
Cm7
C#dim7
cresc.
25
Gm(add2)/D
Cm6/Eb
N.C.
Gm/D
f
29
C7/E
D7/F#
Gm
F13
33
Eb13
Gm
Ebmaj7
p

37
D7
Gm
sfz
Cm7
mf
F7
41
B♭maj7
E♭maj7
Am7♭5
D7
45
Gm
G
Am
B♭dim
G/B
Cm7
f
F7
49
B♭maj7
E♭maj7
Am7♭5
D
p
53
Gm
ff
pp
D7
mf
Gm

57
D7
Gm
D7
Gm
p
mf
61
D
C/E
B♭/F
F♯dim
Gm
f
mp
4
3
65
69
Gm7
E♭/G
Gm
Gdim
73
Gm
Gm(maj7)
Gm
Cm7
cresc.

77
C♯dim7
Gm(add2)/D
Cm6/E♭
N.C.
f
81
Gm/D
C7/E
D7/F♯
Gm
85
F13
E♭13
Gm
p
89
E♭maj7
D7
D7♭5(♭9)
Gm
8va
ff
pp
93
(8va)
rit.
Gm9(maj7)
mf

COME, THOU LONG-EXPECTED JESUS

Music by ROWLAND HUGH PRICHARD
Arranged by Phillip Keveren

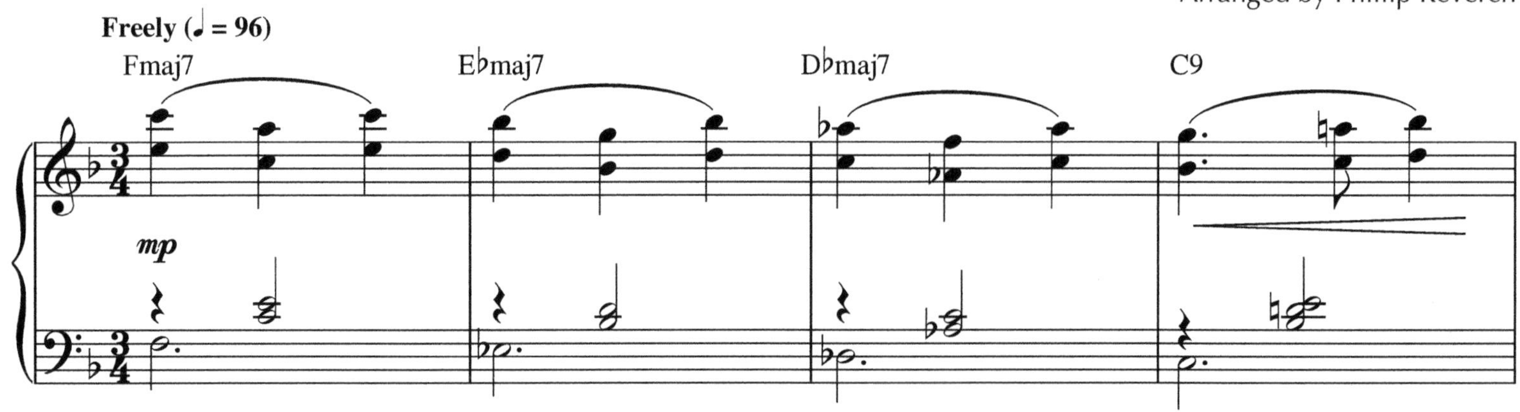

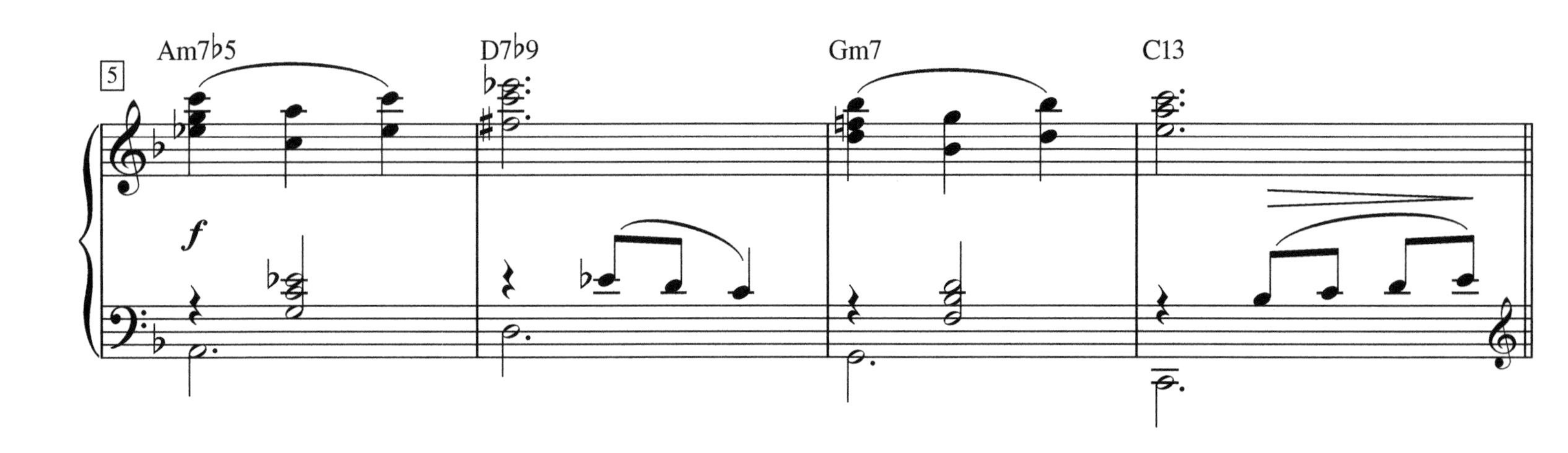

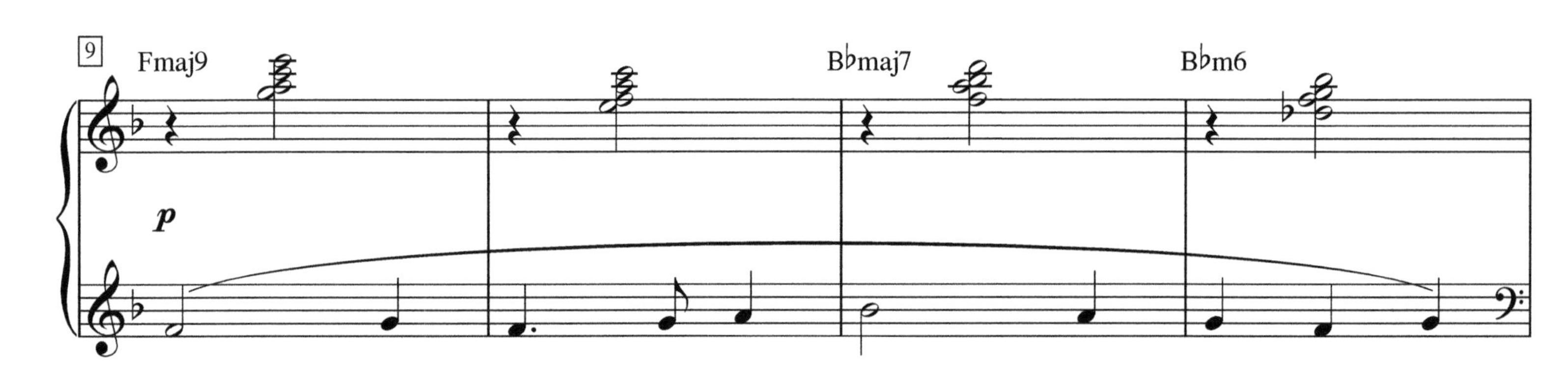

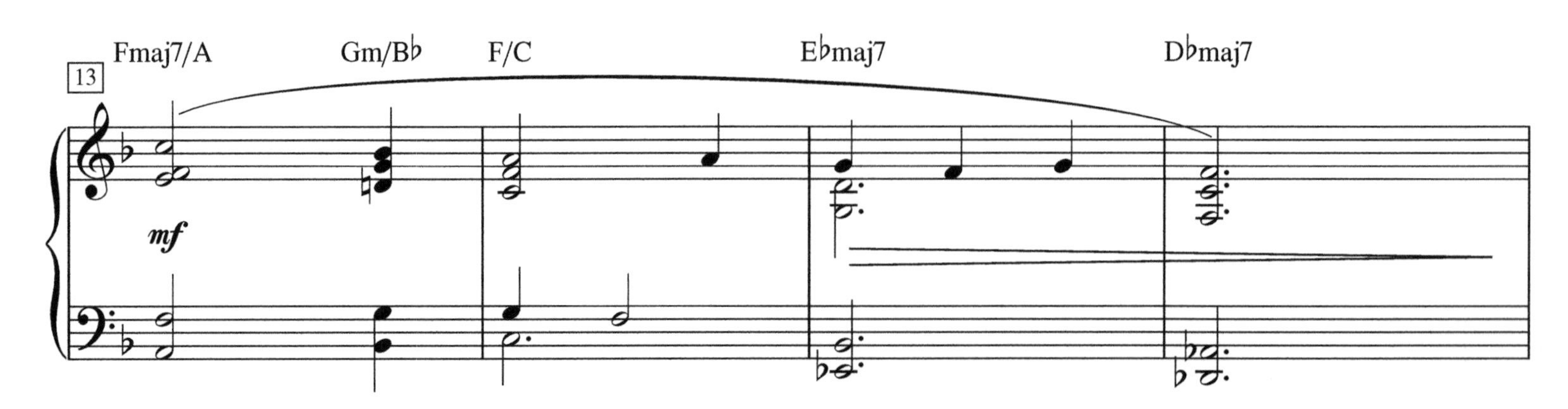

17
F/C
E♭/C
D♭/C
E♭/C
F/C
G♭/C
F/C
E♭/C
D♭/C
E♭/C
p cresc.
21
D♭6/9
C♭6/9
B♭6/9
A♭6/9
G♭6/9
Fmaj9
E♭13
mf
F
Am7
D7
Gm7
C9
25
3
mp
E♭7♭5
D7
Gm7
C9
30
F9
E♭9
F9♯5
E♭9♯11
34
pp

F(add2)/A F/A Am Bbmaj7 F(add2)/A Eb(add2)/G A/F Dm/F Gm7/C C7b9
38
f
Am9 Am7/D D7b9 G(add2) Em9 Am9
42
Am7/D D/C Bm9 Em7(add4) Cmaj7 D/E Cmaj7/D
47
G(add2) G+ C(add2)/G Cm6/G Bm9
52
mp
cresc.
F9#11 Eb9 Db9#11 Bb/C Ab13
57
f

E♭13
D9
C♯m7♭5
F13
62
Am9
Am7/D
D13♯11
Gmaj7/D
Fmaj7/D
66
rit.
mf a tempo
Gmaj7/D
G+/D
Am7/D
G(add2)/B
G/B
Bm
Cmaj7
G(add2)/B
F(add2)/A
71
f
B/G
Em/G
Am7/D
D7♭9
Cm(add2)/G
G
Bm/D
75
rit. e dim.
p cresc.
Am/D
G/D
D7♭9
G6/9
79
mf
pp

DANCE OF THE SUGAR PLUM FAIRY/ GOD REST YE MERRY, GENTLEMEN

Arranged by Phillip Keveren

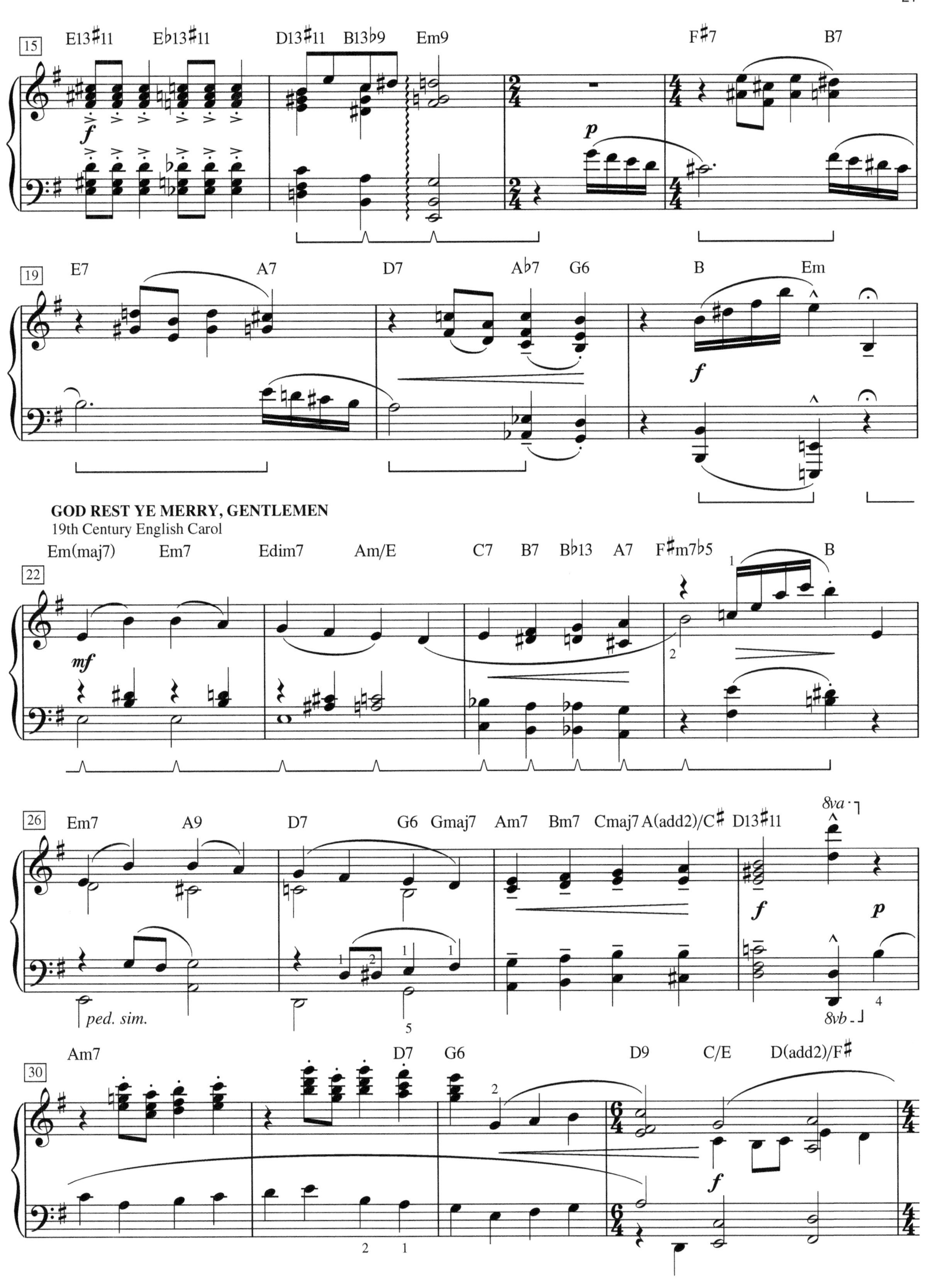
15
E13♯11
E♭13♯11
D13♯11
B13♭9
Em9
F♯7
B7
f
p
19
E7
A7
D7
A♭7
G6
B
Em
f
GOD REST YE MERRY, GENTLEMEN
19th Century English Carol
Em(maj7)
Em7
Edim7
Am/E
C7
B7
B♭13
A7
F♯m7♭5
B
22
mf
26
Em7
A9
D7
G6
Gmaj7
Am7
Bm7
Cmaj7
A(add2)/C♯
D13♯11
8va
f
p
ped. sim.
8vb
30
Am7
D7
G6
D9
C/E
D(add2)/F♯
f

Gmaj7
Am7
Gmaj7
F♯m7♭5
B7
E13
G(add2)/B
G♭(add2)/B♭
Am7
34
A♭13♭9
C/D
D7♭9
Gmaj7
F♯m7♭5
B7
37
rit.
Em
Fdim7/E
C13♭9
F7♯9
40
p a tempo
Em
F♯m7♭5
Em6
F♯7
C7
Cdim7
E7
B♭7
B♭dim7
43
D7
A♭7
Gmaj7
F13
Em6
Bmaj7/E
8va
46
rit.
f

DECK THE HALL

Traditional Welsh Carol
Arranged by Phillip Keveren

13
Eb/C F/C Gb/C
F/C Gb/C Ab/C
p
cresc.
1
16
Am/C Bm7b5 Am7 Ab13#11 Bb13#11 B13#11 Bb13#11 Db13#11 C13
f
18
F6/9 Eb13 F6/9 Eb13#11 F6/9 Eb13
mf
f
21
Bbmaj7 Am7 D7b9 G9 C7b9 F6 N.C.
p
4
24
mf
1

27
G
Dm/F
E7♭9
F♯m7♭5
B7♯5
B7
sub. f
mf
30
Em11
D(add2)/C
Em11
33
Cmaj9
Em11
C(add♯4)
36
Em9
C(add♯4)
Em11
39
C(add♯4)
Em11
C

42
Ebmaj7
Eb7
Fm/Eb
Abm/Eb
Cm9
p
mp
45
Fm7
Gm7
Abmaj7
Bb7
Eb
Db/Bb
Eb/Bb
Fb/Bb
Eb/Bb
Fb/Bb
Gb/Bb
p cresc.
48
Gm/Bb
Am7b5
Gm7
Gb13#11
Ab13#11
A13#11
Ab13#11
B13#11
Bb13
f
50
Eb6/9
Db13
Eb6/9
Db13#11
Eb6/9
Db13
mf
f
53
Am7b5
Gm7
C7b9
F9
Bb7b9
Eb6/9
Eb13#11
ff

DING DONG! MERRILY ON HIGH!

French Carol
Arranged by Phillip Keveren

16
Am7♭5
D7♭9
Gm7
D♭dim7
F7/C
E♭/B♭
F7/A
E♭maj7
B♭(add2)/D
20
Cm7
F7♭9
B♭(add2)
8va
f
Tempo I (𝅗𝅥 = 168)
C
Dm
Em
Dm
mf
24
C
B
B♭6
A7
A♭
G
F♯9♭5
28
C
Dm7
Em7
F
G
Am7
G/B
C
Dm
D♭maj7
D♭7♭5
p cresc.
Tempo II (𝅗𝅥 = 144)
32
C
Em7♭5
Edim7
Dm7
Ddim7
Cmaj7
Am7
f
mf

36
Bm7♭5
E7♭9
Am7
E♭dim7
G7/D
F/C G7/B
Fmaj7
C(add2)/E
40
Dm7
G7♭9
Em7
A7
Dm7
G7
f
43
Cmaj7
Fmaj7
Bm7♭5
E7♯9
Am7
D7
46
G
F(add2)/A
G(add2)/B
Fmaj7
F/G
G13♭9
A♭maj7
rit. e dim.
50
D♭maj7
Cmaj7
mp
pp

THE FIRST NOEL

17th Century English Carol
Music from W. Sandys' *Christmas Carols*
Arranged by Phillip Keveren

Bm9
F♯m7(add4)
Em9
Bm9
17
Em9
F♯m7
Gmaj7
Dmaj9/A
B♭
C
21
D
A13
D6/A
Bm7
A(add2)/C♯
A/C♯
D(add2)/F♯
Gmaj7
G6
25
mf
F♯m7
Dmaj7/F♯
Bm9
A/G
D/F♯
Em7
29
3
F♯(add2)
A13♭9
Bm/F♯
F♯m
33
pp

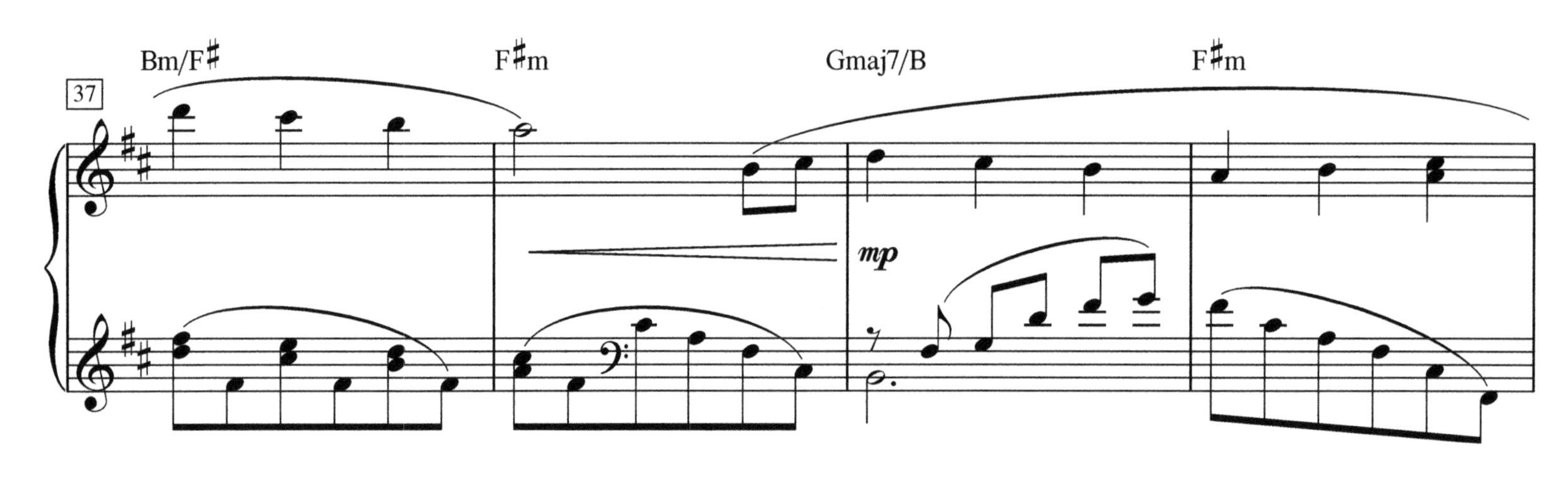
Bm/F♯
F♯m
Gmaj7/B
F♯m
37
mp

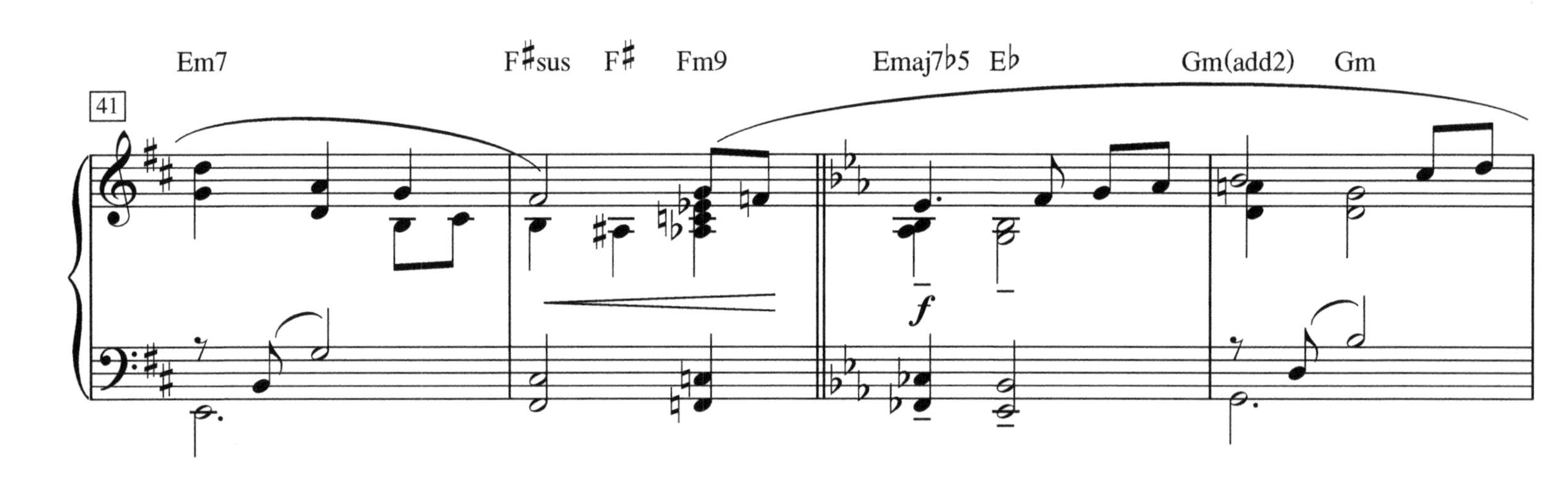
Em7
F♯sus
F♯
Fm9
Emaj7♭5
E♭
Gm(add2)
Gm
41
f

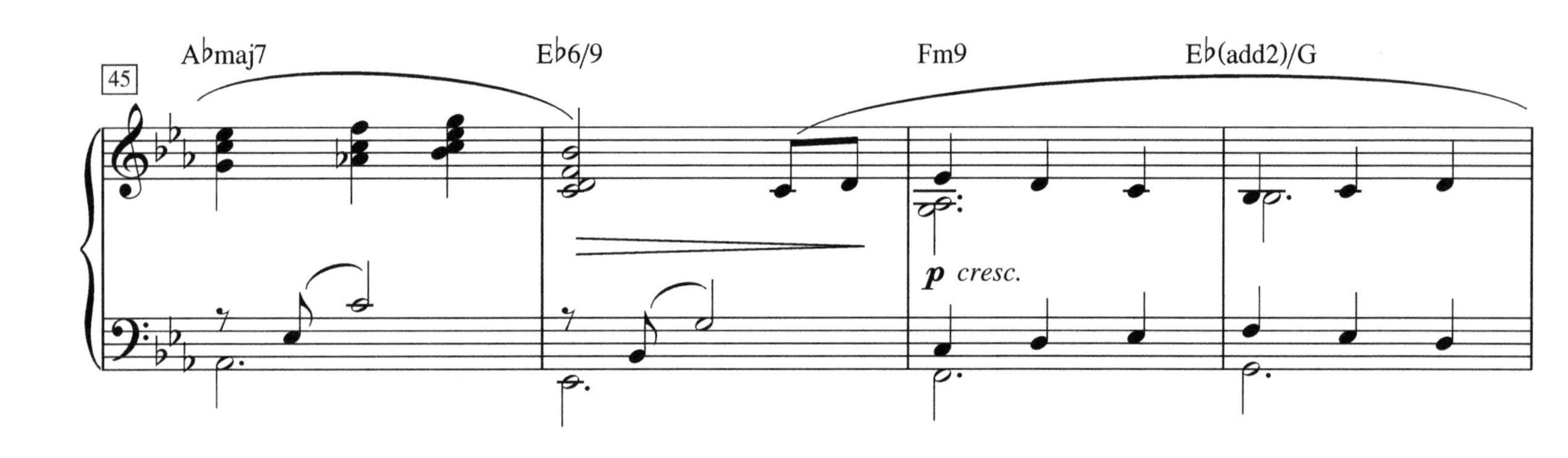
A♭maj7
E♭6/9
Fm9
E♭(add2)/G
45
p cresc.

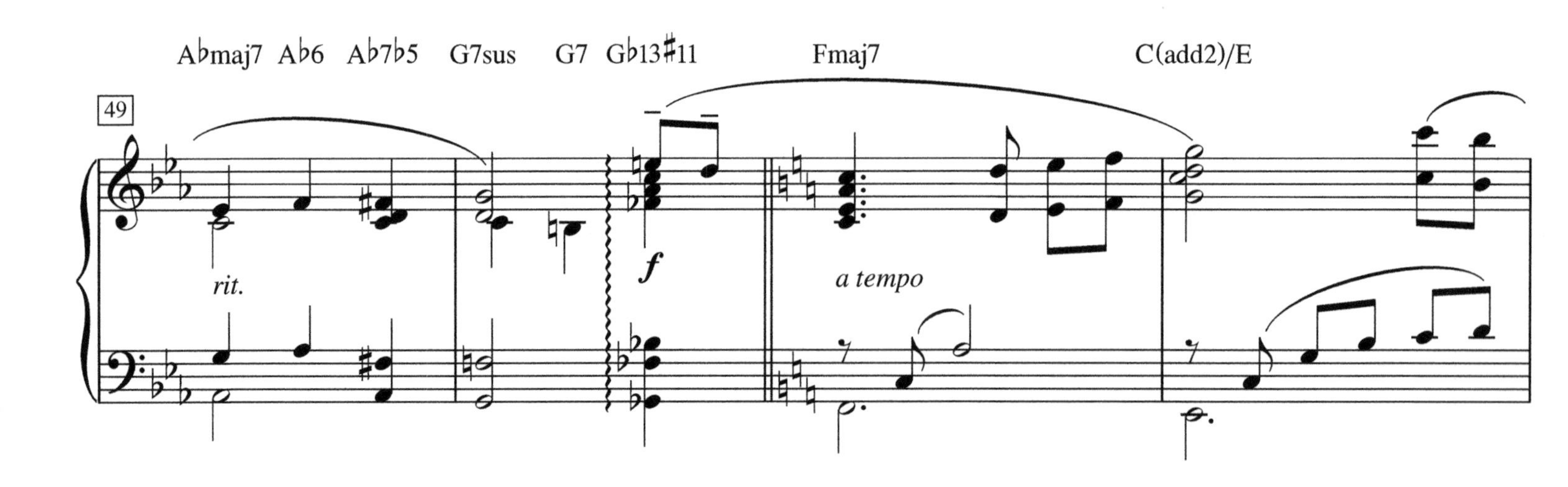
A♭maj7
A♭6
A♭7♭5
G7sus
G7
G♭13♯11
Fmaj7
C(add2)/E
49
rit.
f
a tempo

Boldly (♩ = 84)
F
C
G/B
Am
G/A
F/A
Em
53
broaden
ff
molto rit.
Tempo I
F/G
Em/G
Fm/G
C
E/C
57
p
D/C
Cm7
Em7♭5
A7♭9
61
mf
Dm7
G7♭9
C6/9
C6/9(add♯4)
C6/9
65
rit. e dim.
pp

HERE WE COME A-WASSAILING

Traditional
Arranged by Phillip Keveren

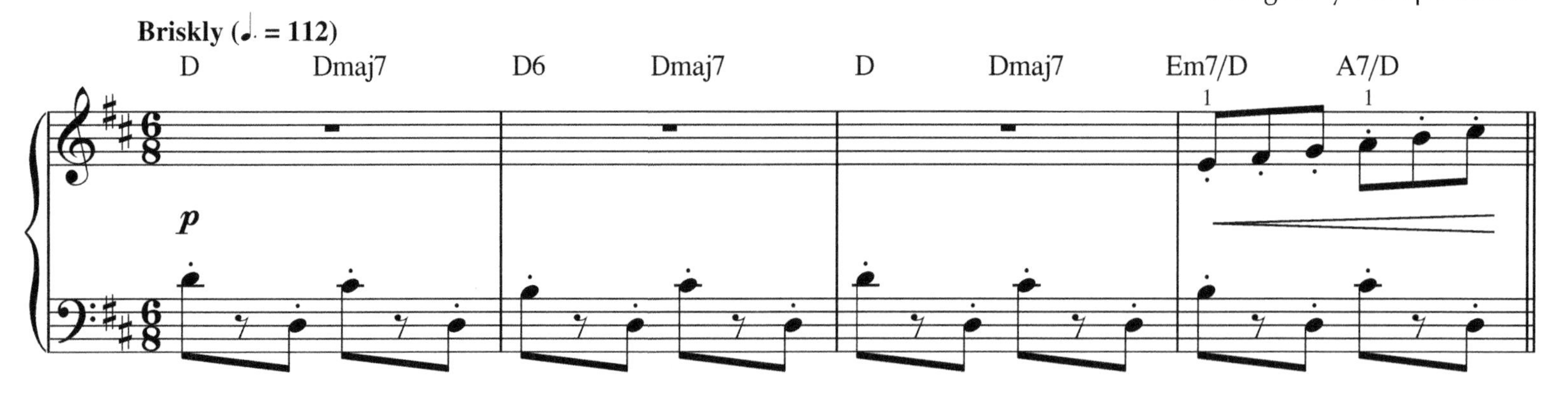

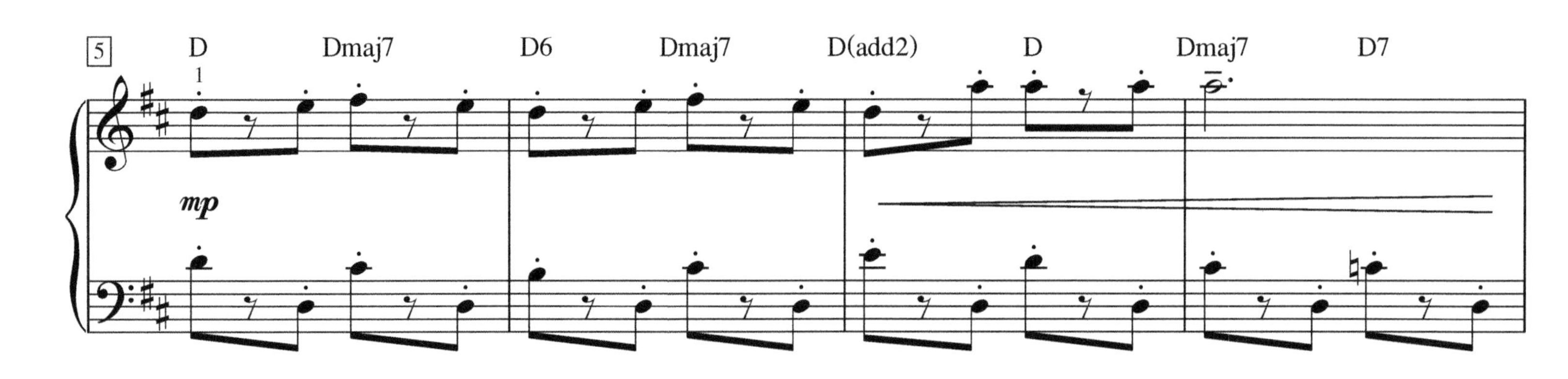

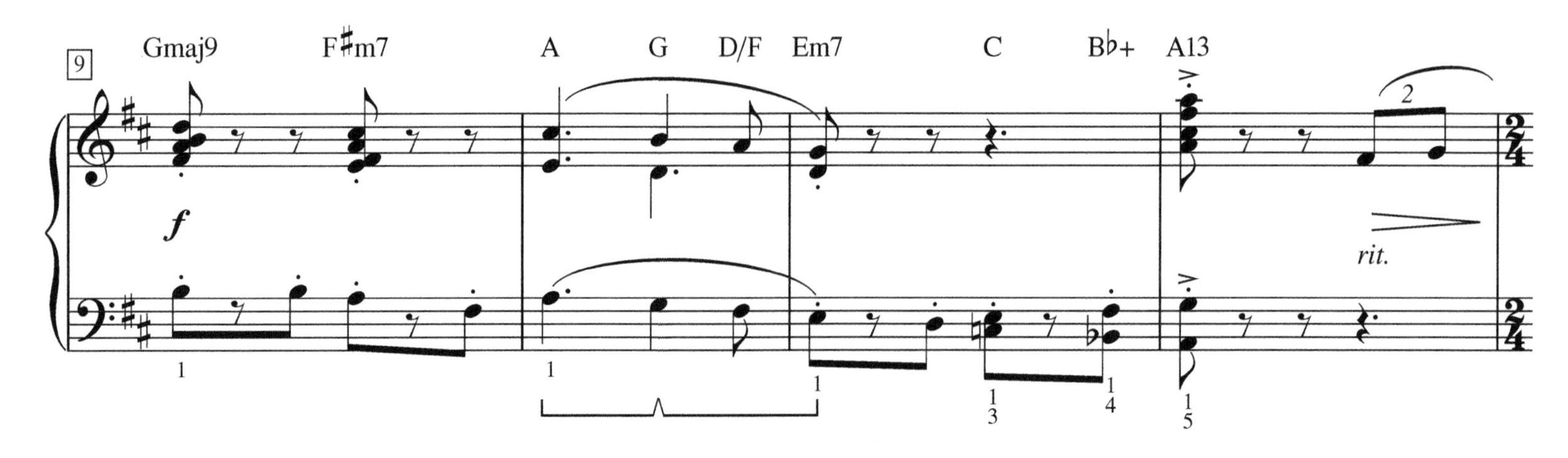

18
Em7 A7sus A7 Bm Gm6/B♭ A13 F♯m7♭5 B7♭9 Em7 Gm/AA7♭9
rit.
Tempo I
23
E♭maj7 D Dmaj9 Dm Dm(maj7) Dm7 Dm(maj7) Dm Dm(maj7)
p
28
C/D A7/D Dm Dm(maj7) Dm7 Dm(maj7) Dm Dm(maj7)
mp
32
Dm7 G/D Gm6/B♭ B♭maj7/A Dm/A C♯dim7
f
Slower, freely (♩ = 96)
36
A7♯5 C9 C13 Fmaj9 B♭maj7/F C/E B♭/D Fmaj7/C B♭(add2)/D
rit.
mf warmly

C(add2)/E C13 Am7 D Gm7 C7sus C7 Dm B♭m6/D♭ C13
41
Deliberately (♩ = 72)
Am7♭5 D7♭9 Gm7 B♭m/C C7♭9 F/A A♭dim7 Gm9 G♭9 F6/9 E♭13 D13
46
broaden
f
D♭6/9 B♭maj7/C F6/9/C D♭/E♭ D♭13♯11 C13♯11 Am7 D7♭9 Gm7 B♭maj7/C C7
51
F/C B♭m6/D♭ F/C D7 Gm7 Am7 B♭maj7 C7♯5
56
freely
ff
mf
F(add2) F6/9
60
p

THE HOLLY AND THE IVY

18th Century English Carol
Arranged by Phillip Keveren

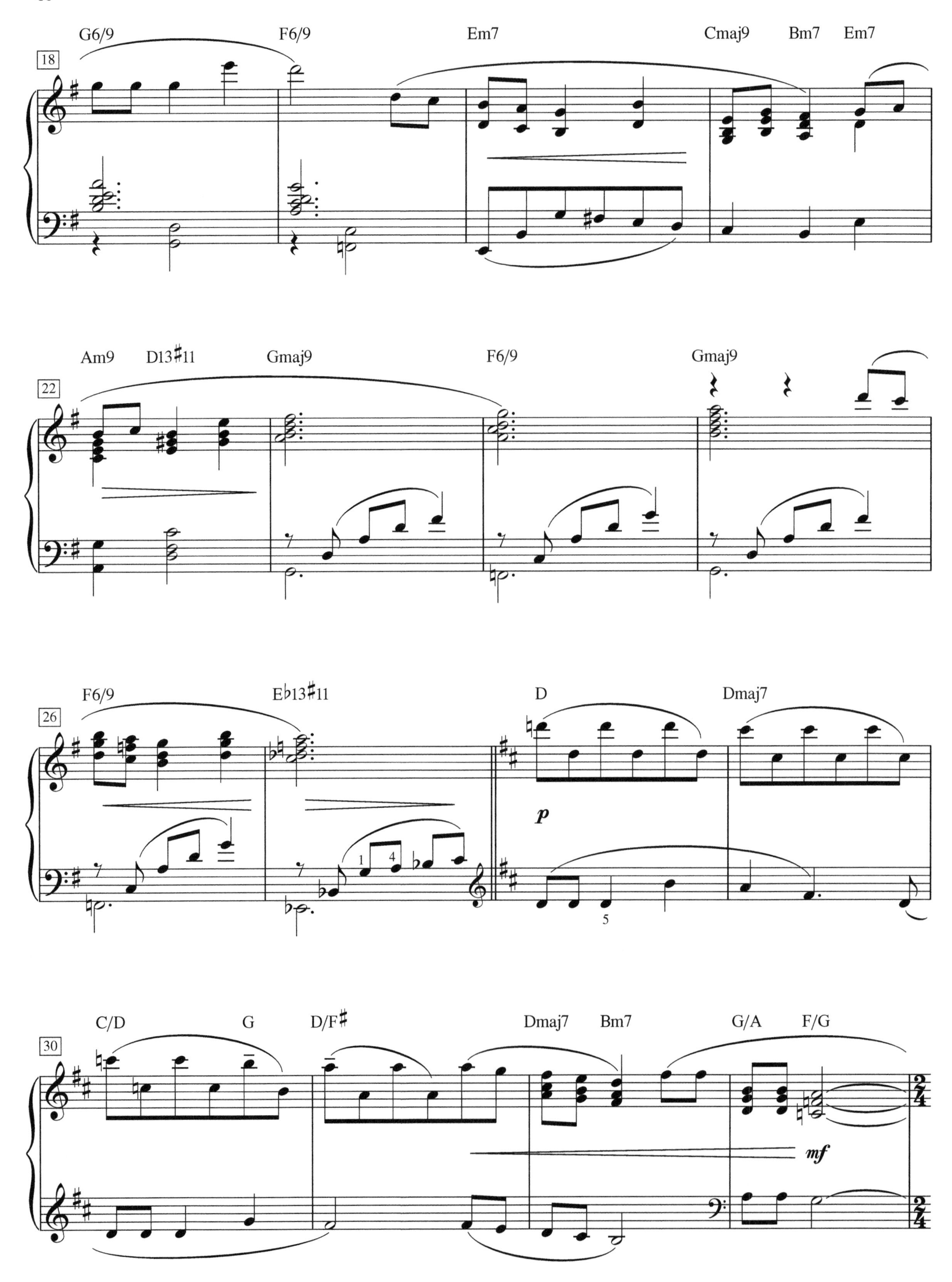
18
G6/9
F6/9
Em7
Cmaj9
Bm7
Em7
22
Am9
D13#11
Gmaj9
F6/9
Gmaj9
26
F6/9
E♭13#11
D
Dmaj7
p
30
C/D
G
D/F#
Dmaj7
Bm7
G/A
F/G
mf

34
Gmaj7
A
B♭
B♭7
E♭6/9
p
f
38
D♭6/9
Cm7
A♭maj7(add4)
Fm7
E♭(add2)/G
A♭maj7
42
D♭maj7
E♭
A♭m/C♭
Gm/B♭
Fm9
B♭13♯9
E♭6/9
dim.
46
D♭6/9
E♭6/9
D♭6/9
C6/9
A/C
rit.
mp
pp

I HEARD THE BELLS ON CHRISTMAS DAY

Music by JOHN BAPTISTE CALKIN
Arranged by Phillip Keveren

16
E7
E♭6
E♭6/9
A♭maj7
E♭6/9
p
20
D♭6/9
Cmaj7
F/C
D♯m7
f
23
Em7
C/E
G/F
Fmaj7
F/G
G13
B(♯5)
B♭(♭5)
A♭(♯5)
G♭(♭5)
p
f
27
Em/G
F/G
G
Am/G
G7
C/G
C(add2)/G
p cresc.
30
Dmaj7/A
A7sus
A7
G/A
Gm/A

Dmaj7
D♭maj7 Dmaj7
F13
Em7
D♯m7 Em7
Fdim7
D(add2)/F♯
33
f
G(add2)
A13
G(add2)
Dmaj7/A
36
mf
F♯/A♯
F♯
Bm
Gm6/B♭
F♯m/A
A9/G
D/F♯
Em11
A13♭9
N.C.
39
f
D
Em
F♯m
G
A/G
Em
F♯m
G
A
Dmaj9/F♯
43
p
mp
Em7
D(add2)/F♯
Gmaj7
Gm6/A
Dmaj7
Dmaj7(add♯4)
47
mf
f
p

IN THE BLEAK MIDWINTER

Music by GUSTAV HOLST
Arranged by Phillip Keveren

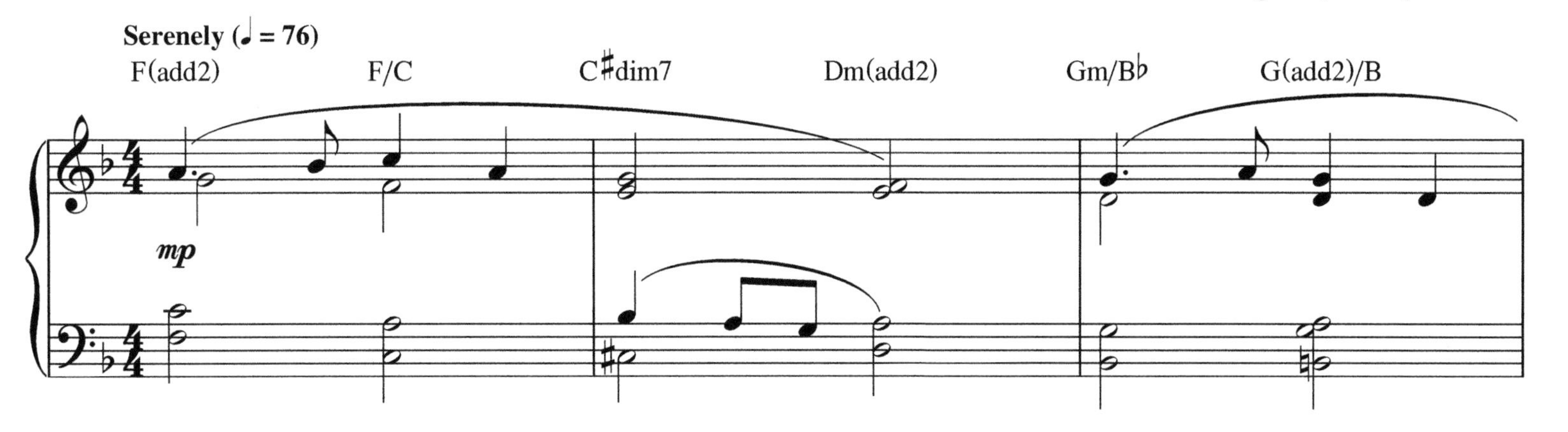

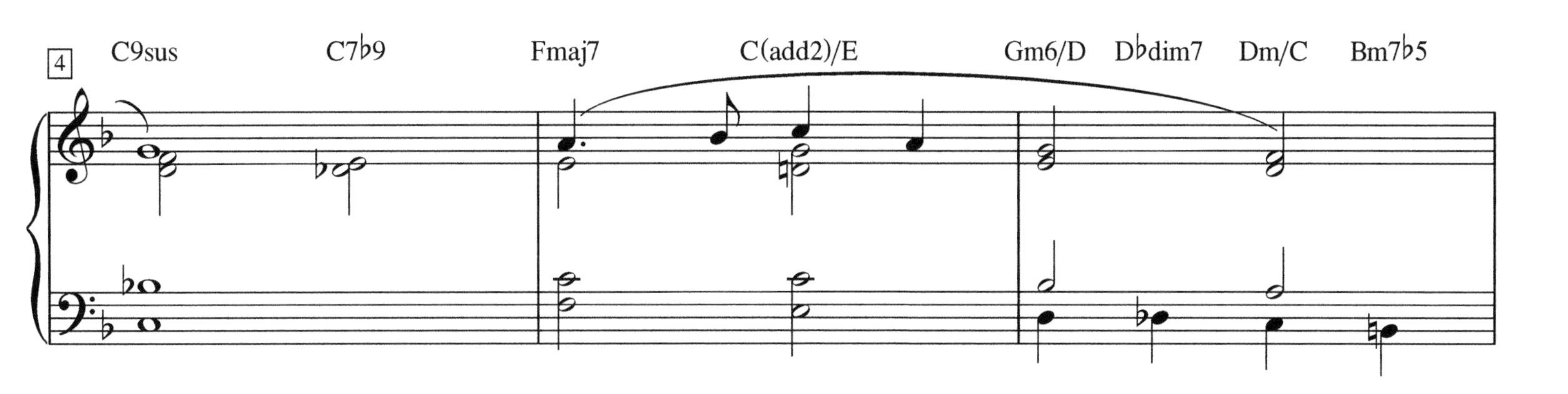

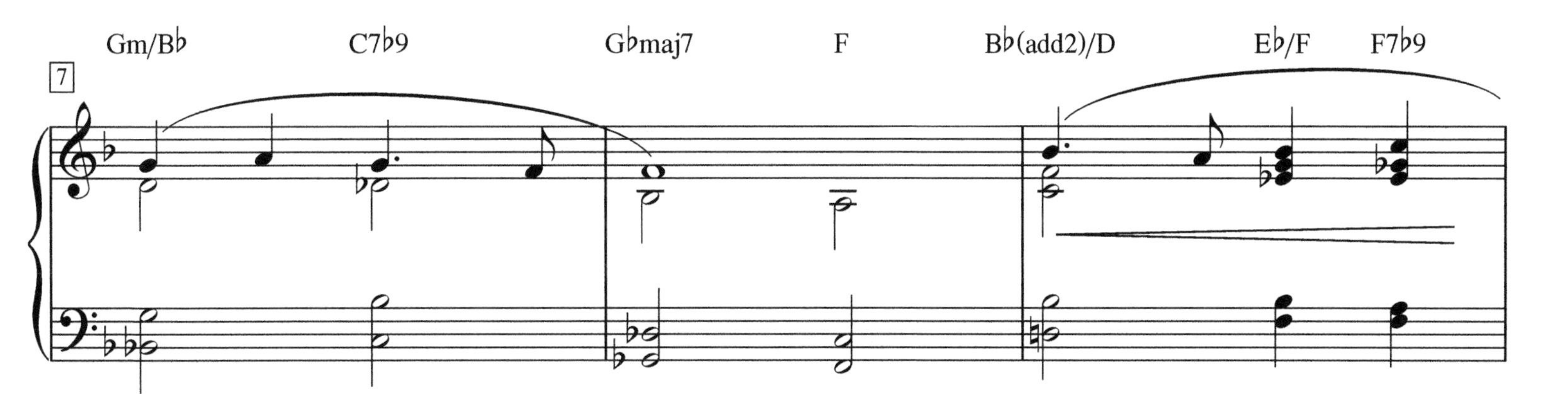

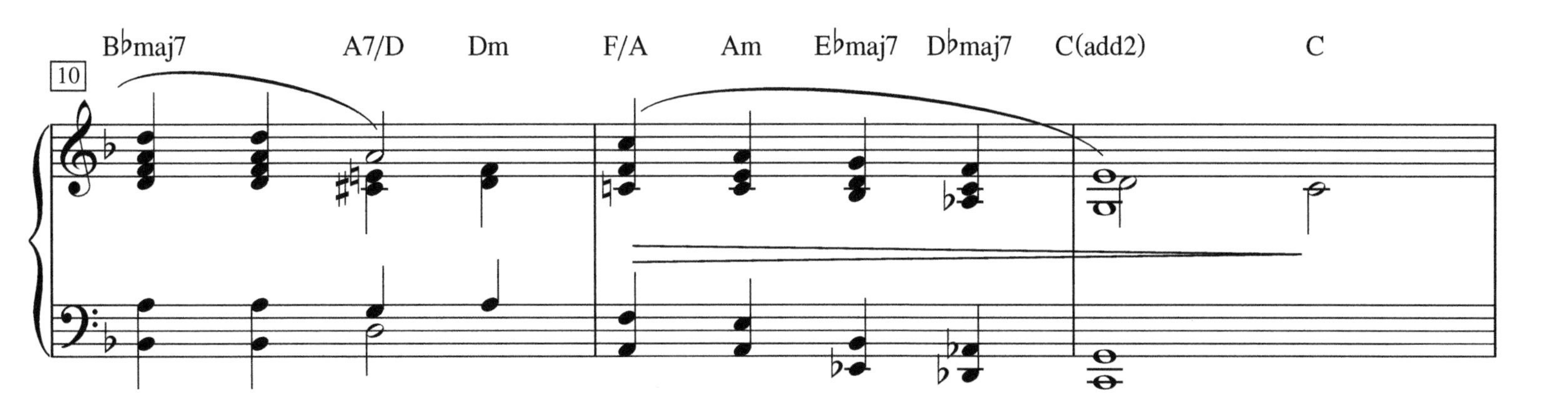

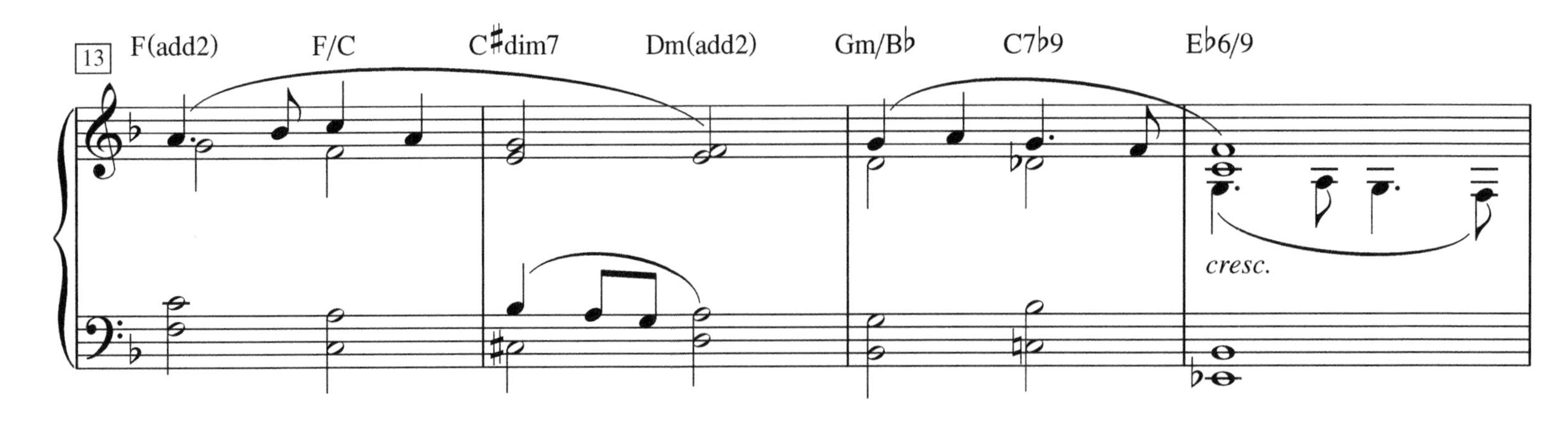
13
F(add2)
F/C
C♯dim7
Dm(add2)
Gm/B♭
C7♭9
E♭6/9
cresc.

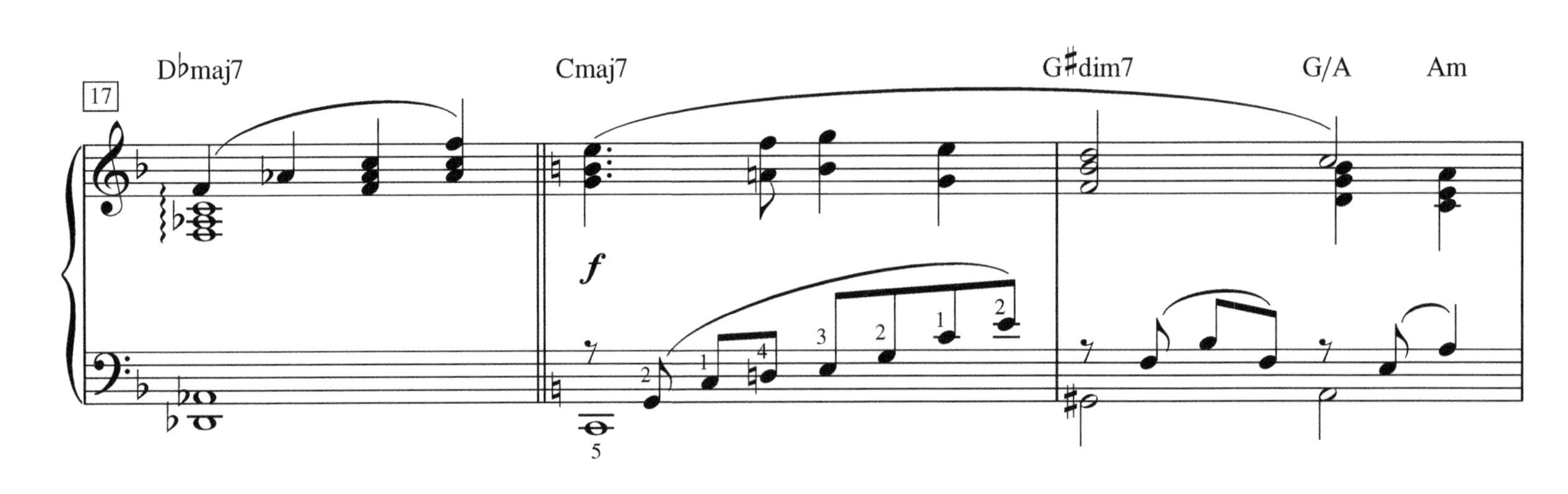
17
D♭maj7
Cmaj7
G♯dim7
G/A
Am
f

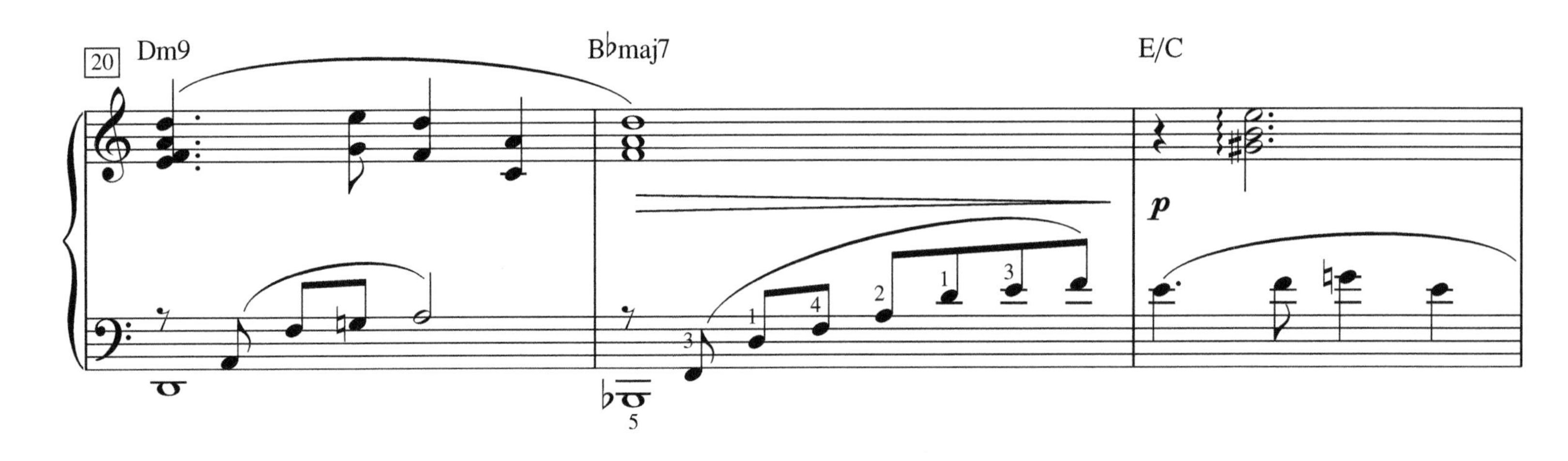
20
Dm9
B♭maj7
E/C
p

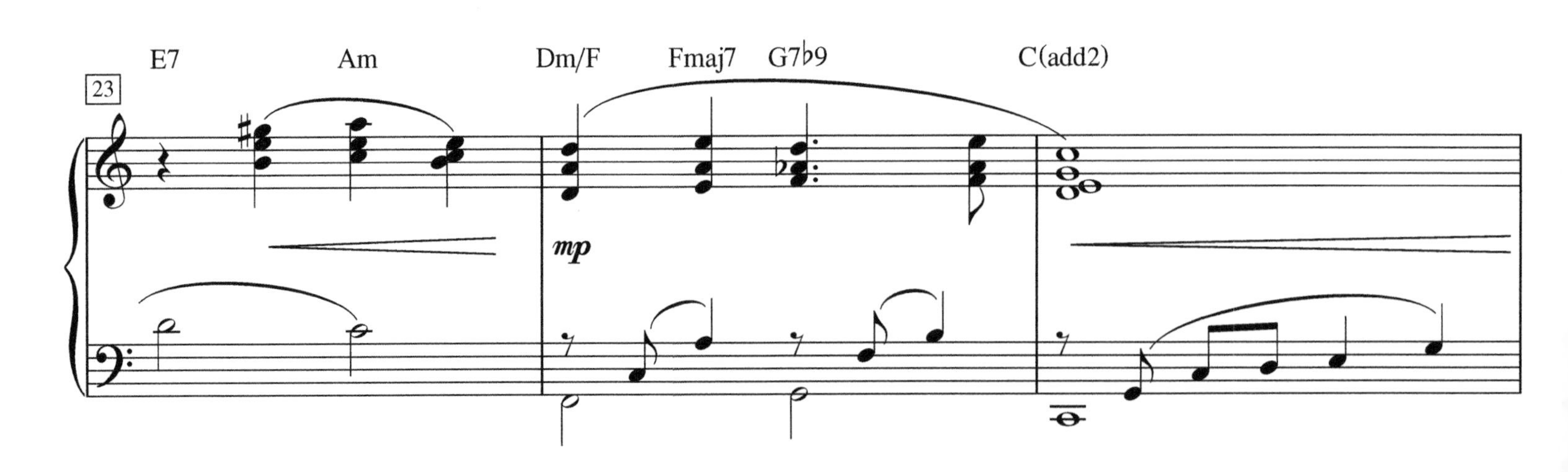
23
E7
Am
Dm/F
Fmaj7
G7♭9
C(add2)
mp

F6/9
Eb9#11
Bb13#11
Am9
D13
D9
26
f
Dm7/G
C
Dm
Eb
G
G#dim7
Am(add2)
29
mf
Dm/F
Fm6/G
Abmaj7
32
accel.

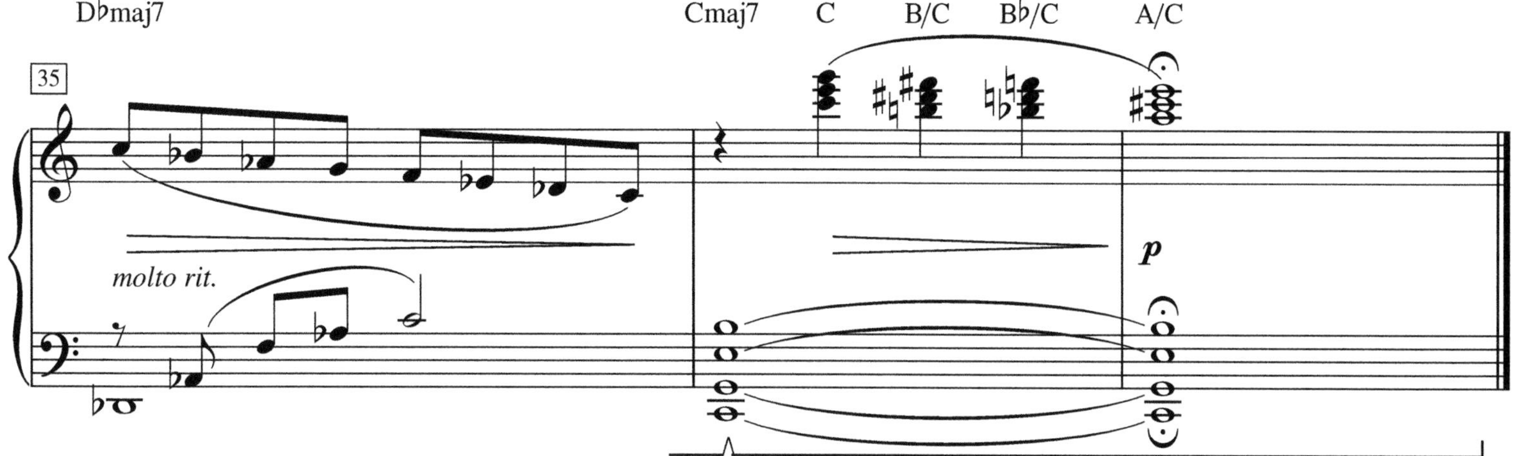
Dbmaj7
Cmaj7
C
B/C
Bb/C
A/C
35
molto rit.
p

JOY TO THE WORLD/ HOW GREAT OUR JOY!

Arranged by Phillip Keveren

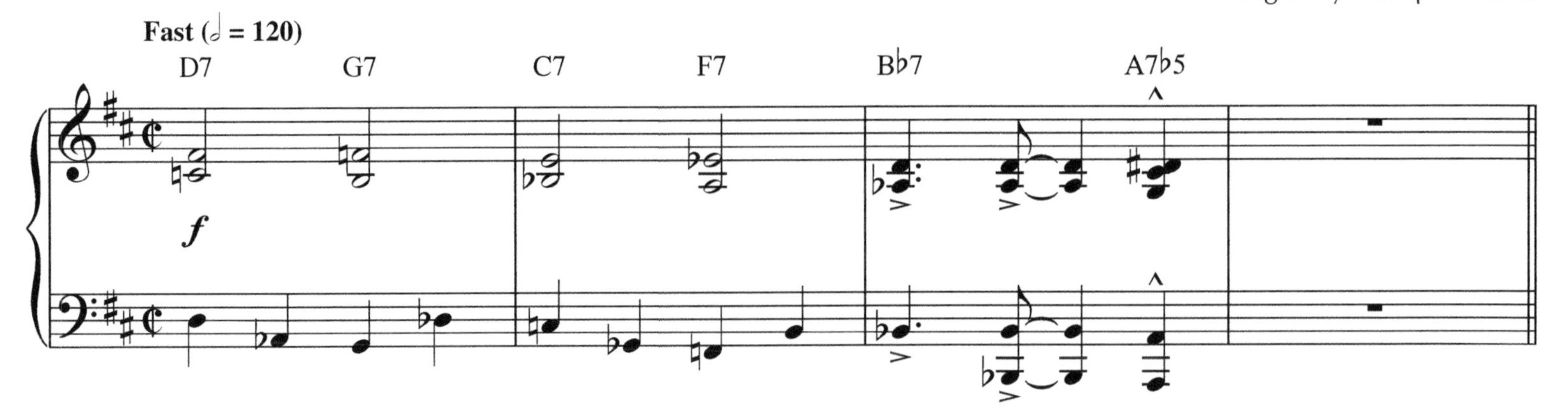

JOY TO THE WORLD
Music by GEORGE FRIDERIC HANDEL
Adapted by LOWELL MASON

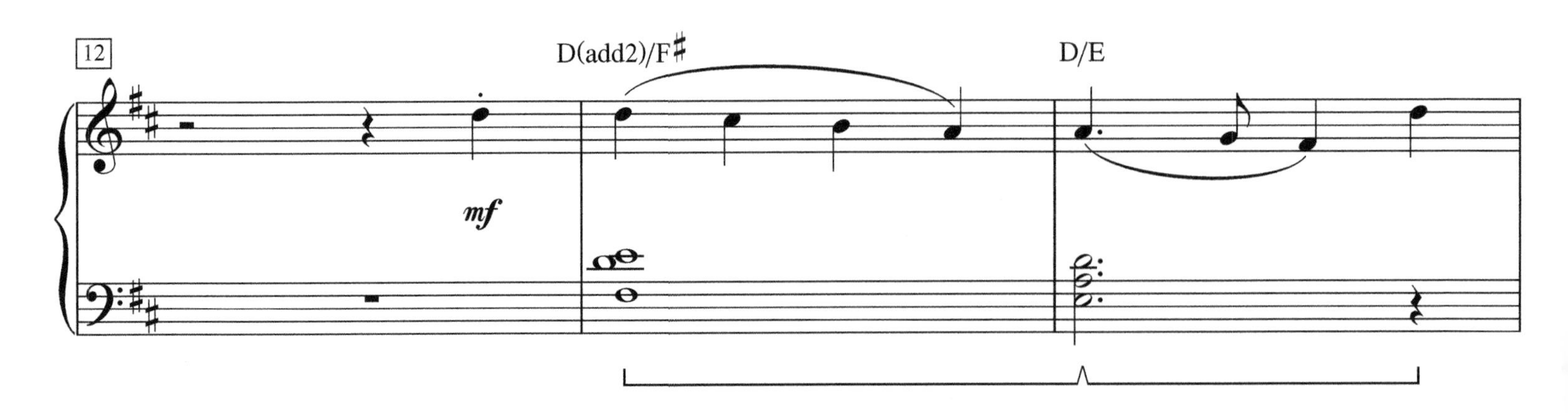

15
Bm7
Gmaj7
3
Dmaj7
D6
p
cresc.
18
F♯m7
B7
4
Em7
B♭m7♭5
3
Am7
5
A7
3
1
2
2
f
21
D
3
2
1
3
E9
A7
1
5
2
1
2
24
D
G7
C7
F7
B♭7
A7♭5
HOW GREAT OUR JOY!
Traditional German Carol
28
D
E/D
F♯/D
B♭/D

32
D
Em
A7
D
36
D♯7♭9
Bm7
Dmaj7
E(add2)
p
40
Bm7
A9
Dmaj7
C9
A/B
B♭9♯5
f
p
44
F♯m/A
C♯m7♭5
Dmaj7
Em7
F♯7♭9
Bm7
f
47
N.C.
F♯
Bm6
p
3
3
2
3
1

51
N.C.
sfz
p
mf
55
f
G6
59
A7♭9
D6
62
mf
65
p
cresc.
Dmaj7
D6
F♯m7
B7

68
Em7
B♭m7♭5
Am7
A7
D
f
71
E9
A7
F♯m7♭5
B7♭9
B♭7♯5
A7
75
D
Dmaj7
D7
G/D
Gm/D
79
D
Dmaj7
D7
G/D
Gm/D
83
N.C.
E9
A7
D6

O CHRISTMAS TREE

Traditional German Carol
Arranged by Phillip Keveren

17
F♯m7♭5
B9
Em7♭5
A13♭9
G♭7
C7/F
F
F/C
p
21
C7
C9
G♭/C
F/C
F6/9
mp
25
E♭13♯11
E♭
D
D♭6
C
F
mf
29
F6/9
E♭6/9
D6/9
Gm6/A
p cresc.
33
D
Bm9
C

B♭(add2)
D/A
G♯m7♭5
36
G
A7
A7/D
D
D/A
A7
39
p
E♭/A
D/A
D
C6/9♯11
43
mf
C
B
B♭6
A
A7/D
D
E
D
47
pp

O COME, O COME, EMMANUEL

15th Century French Melody
Arranged by Phillip Keveren

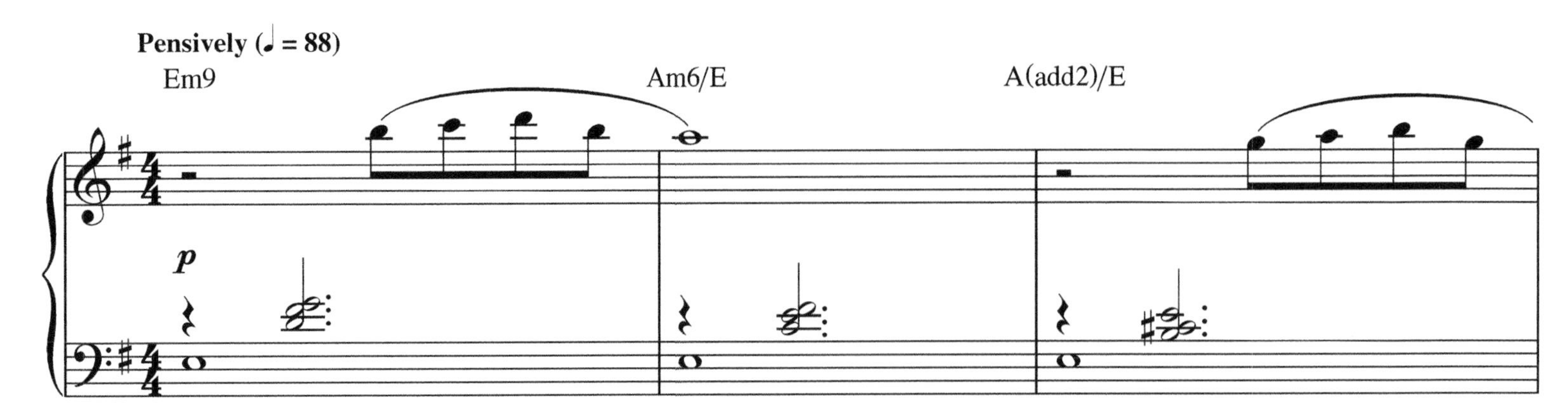

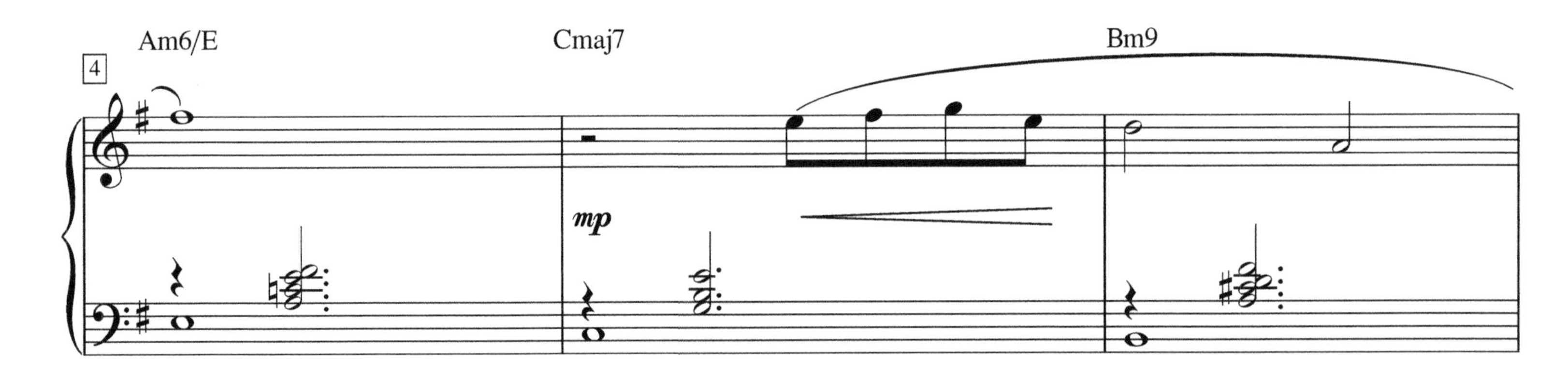

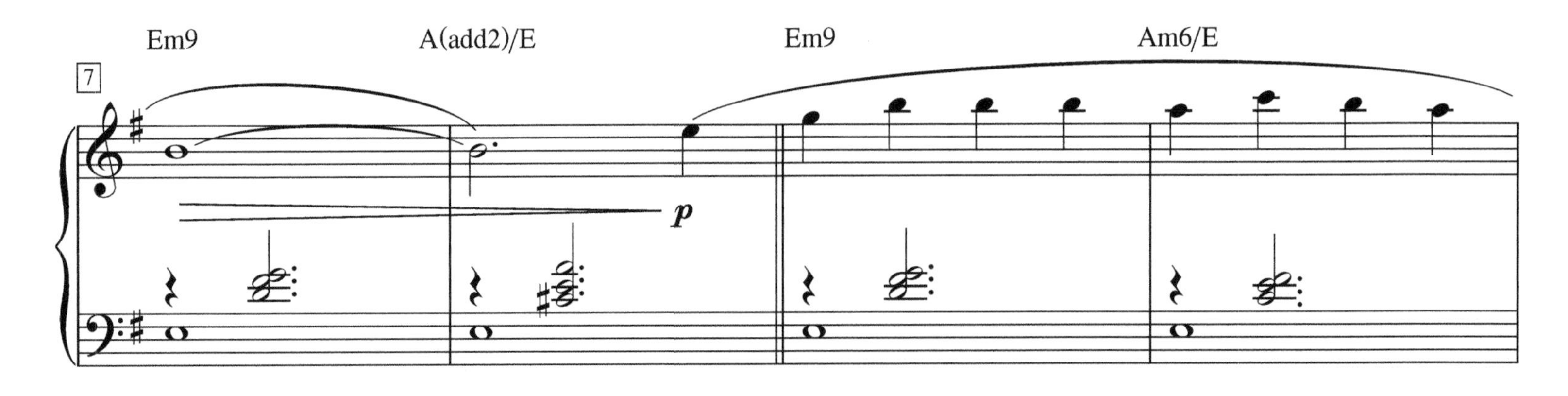

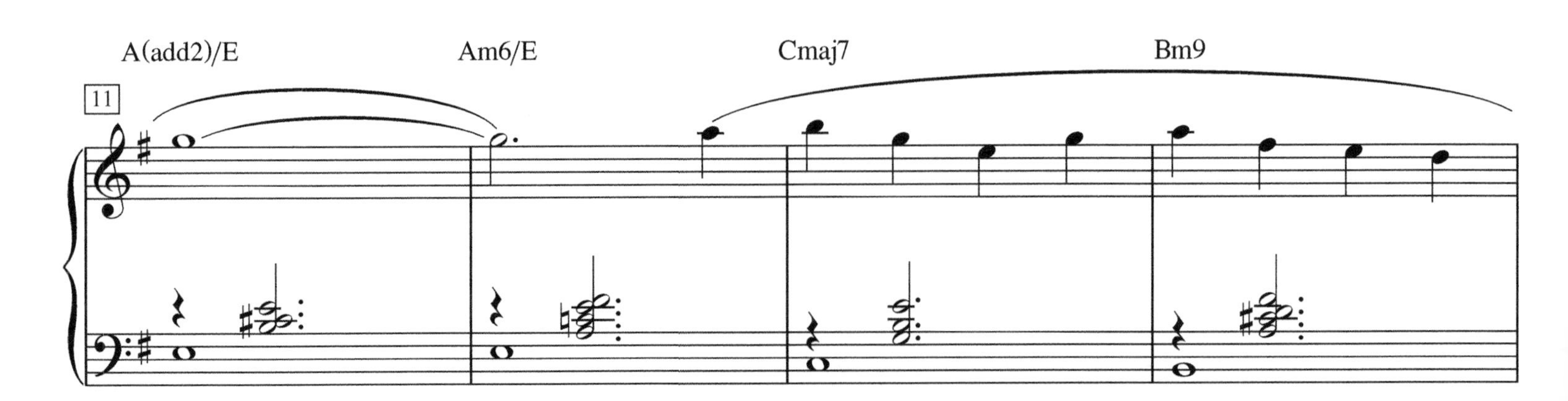

15
Em9
A/E
Am7
Bm7
Cmaj7
D7
mf
19
Em9
Bm7
Em7
Am7
D7♭9
G6
p
cresc.
f
23
Bm9
Em9
Am7
Am/G
F♯m7♭5
B7♭9
26
Em11
D9
Gmaj7
D♭9♯11
Cmaj7
G(add2)/B
Am7
Bm7
29
Em9
Am6/E
A(add2)/E
p

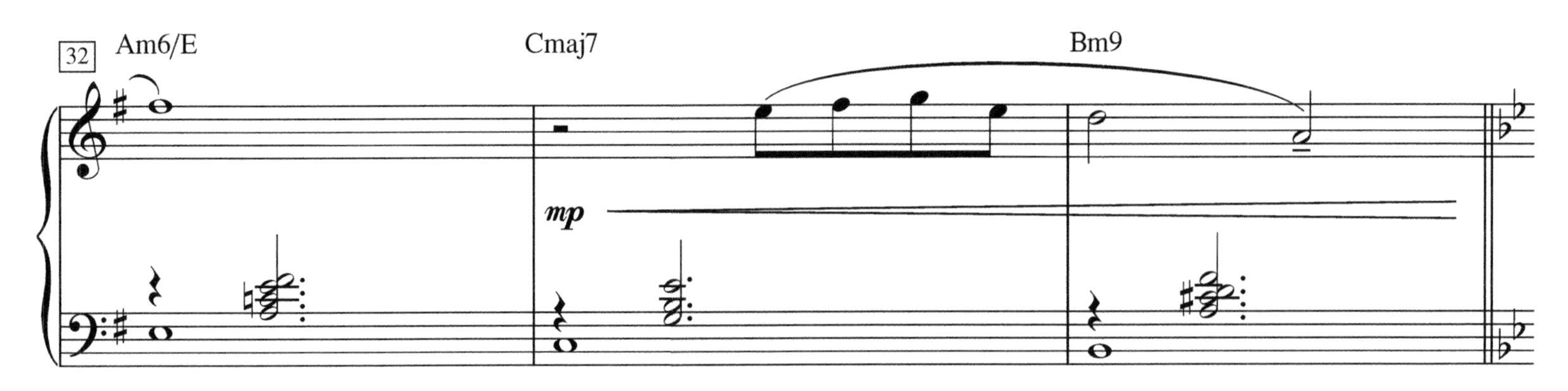
32
Am6/E
Cmaj7
Bm9
mp

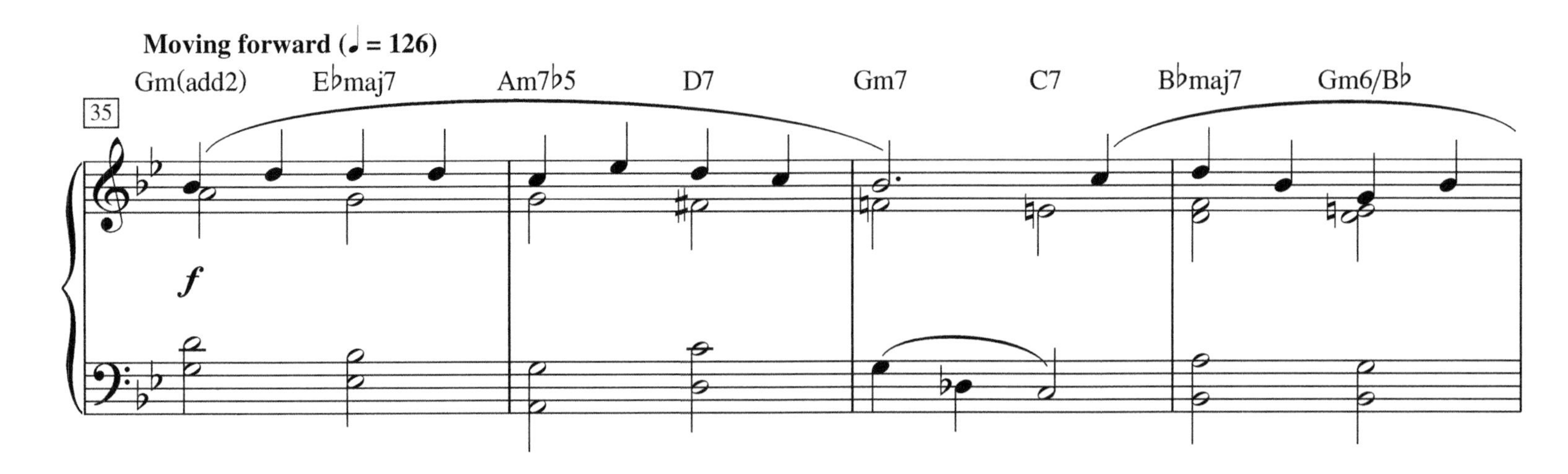
Moving forward (♩ = 126)
Gm(add2)
E♭maj7
Am7♭5
D7
Gm7
C7
B♭maj7
Gm6/B♭
35
f

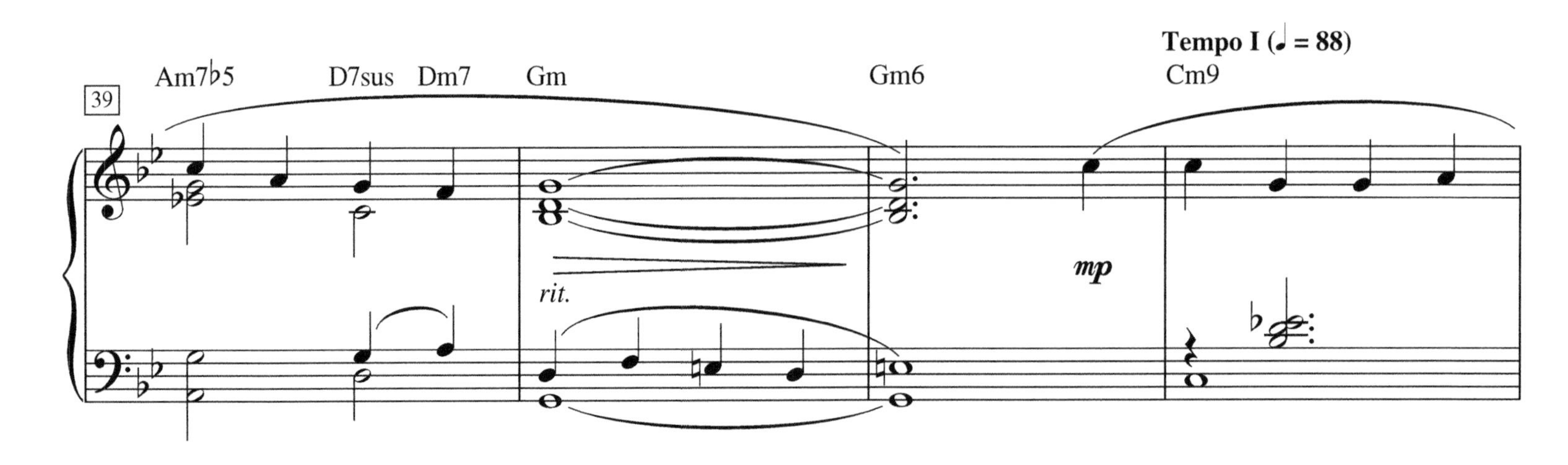
Tempo I (♩ = 88)
Am7♭5
D7sus
Dm7
Gm
Gm6
Cm9
39
rit.
mp

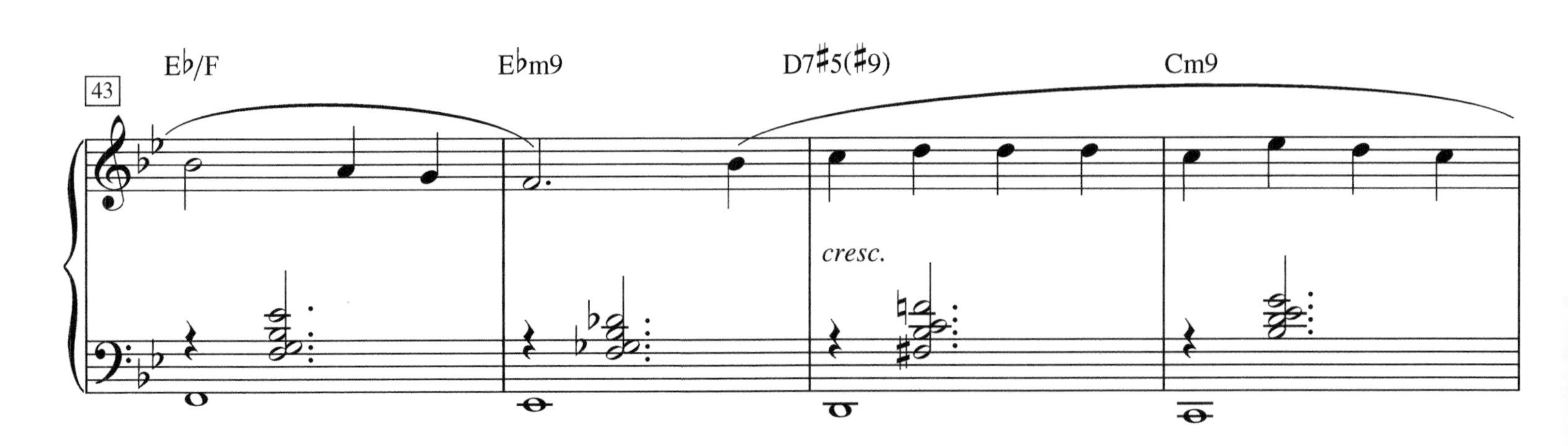
E♭/F
E♭m9
D7♯5(♯9)
Cm9
43
cresc.

47
B♭6/9
E♭maj7
Am7♭5
A♭7♭5
f
mf

51
Gm7
Gm6
E♭maj9
Dm7(add4)
N.C.
p

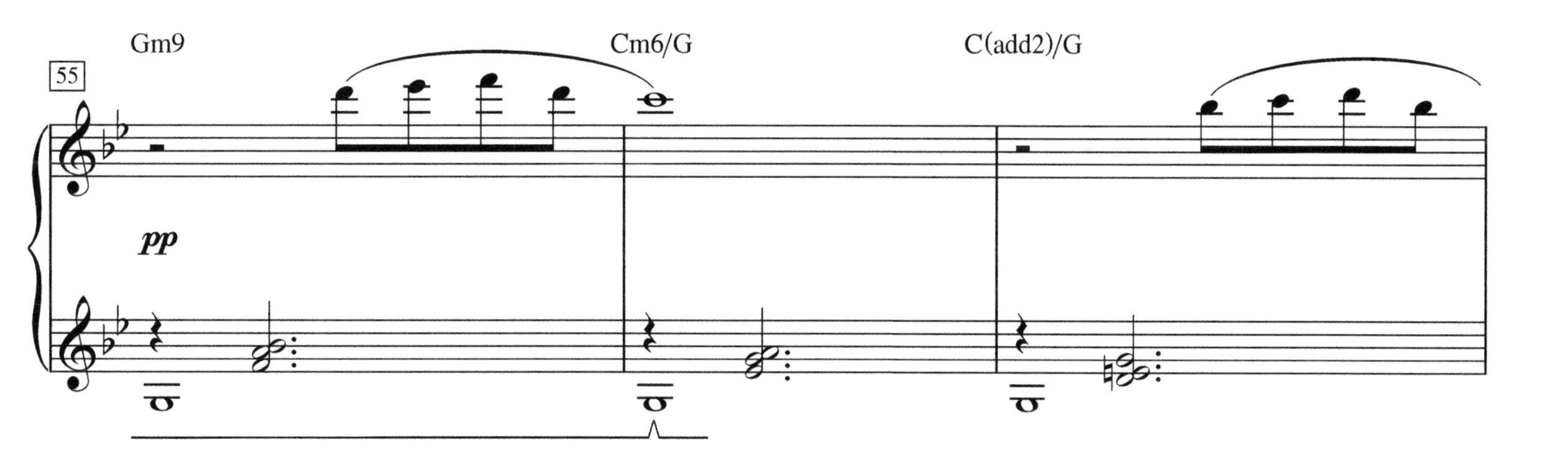
55
Gm9
Cm6/G
C(add2)/G
pp

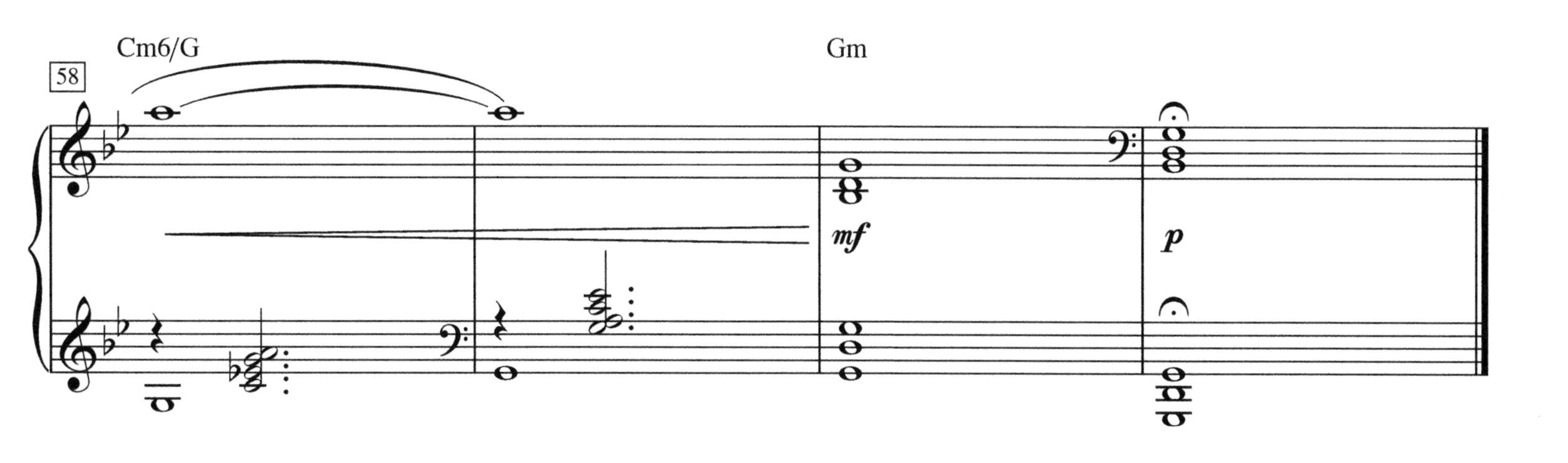
58
Cm6/G
Gm
mf
p

STILL, STILL, STILL

Salzburg Melody, c.1819
Arranged by Phillip Keveren

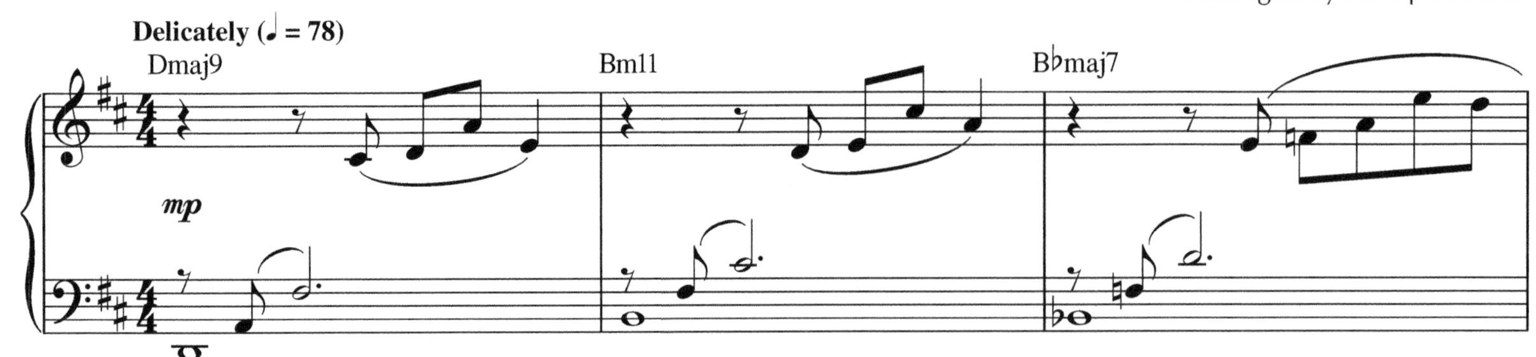

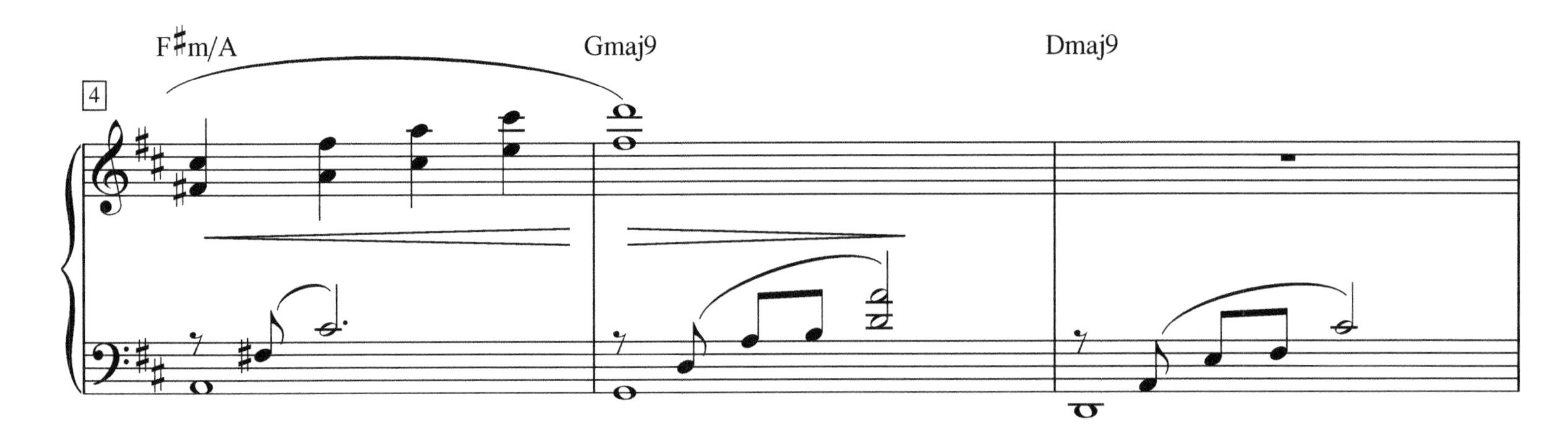

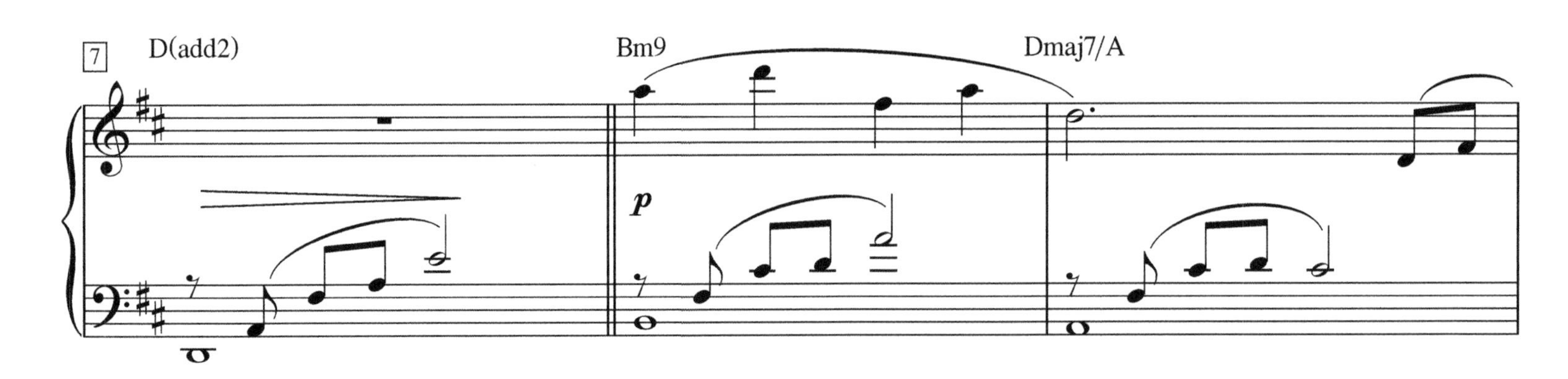

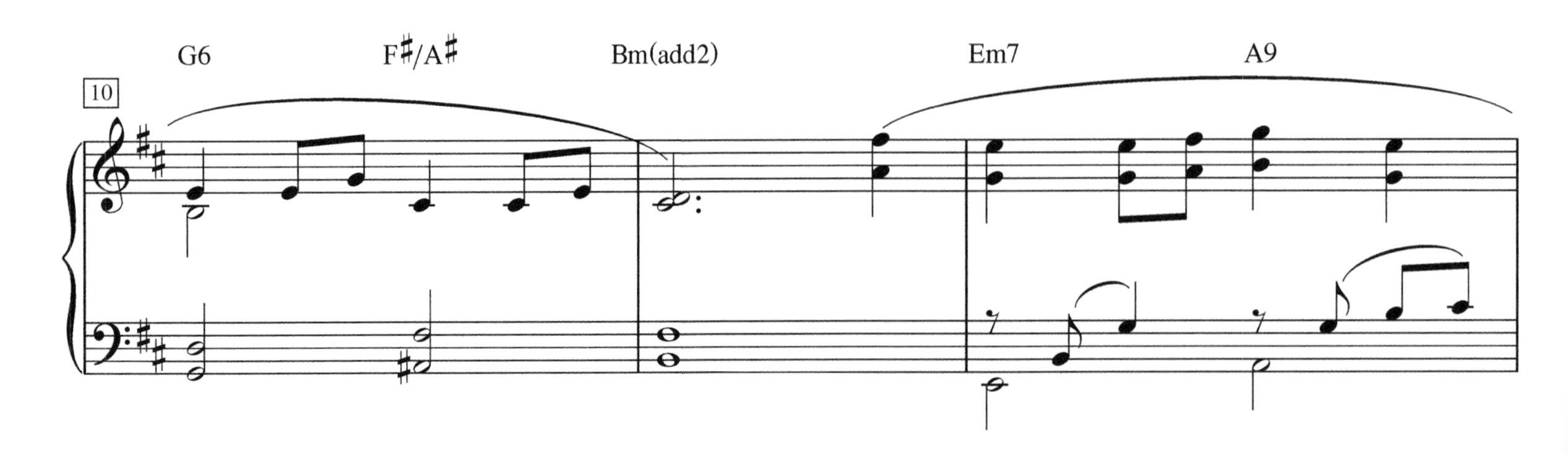

D
D♯dim7
Em7
Cmaj7
Dmaj7
Em7
A7♭9
13
Bm7
D/A
G
D/F♯
16
mp
Gm6/B♭
A9
Dmaj9
Bm11
19
p
B♭maj7
Amaj7
F♯m9
Dmaj9
22
mf
Dm6/F
E7♭9
G(add2)
A(add2)
Em7
25
p

28
F♯m/E
Em9
F♯m11
8va
rit.
pp
8vb
31
F(add2)
B♭(add2)♯4
f a tempo
mf
34
E♭maj7
C(add2)
Fmaj9
p
37
Dm11
D♭maj7
Fmaj7
40
A♭maj7
D♭maj7
Fmaj9
molto rit.

UP ON THE HOUSETOP

Words and Music by
B.R. HANBY
Arranged by Phillip Keveren

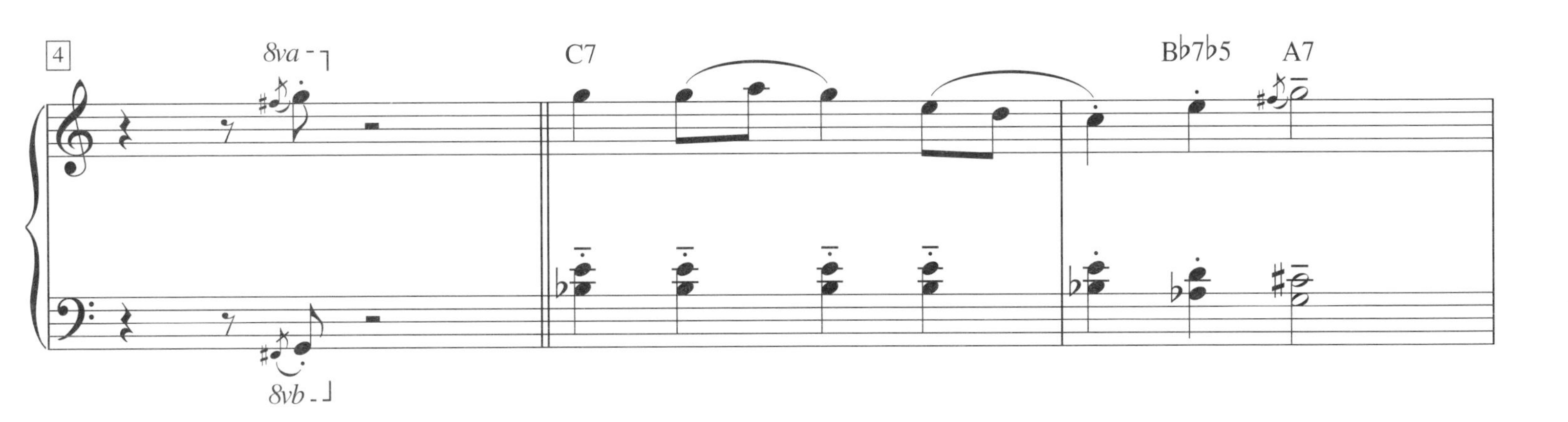

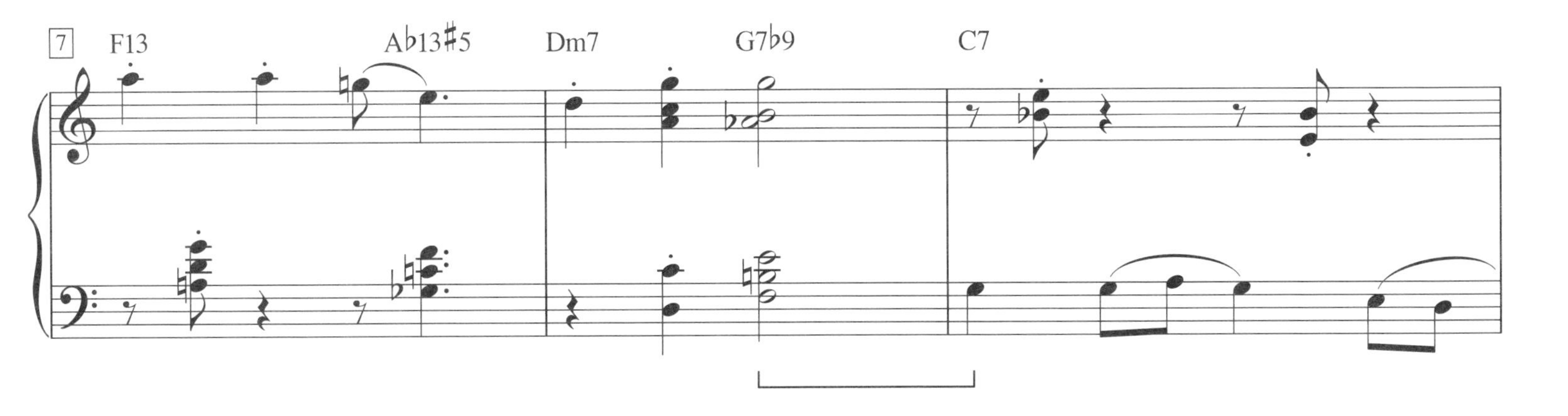

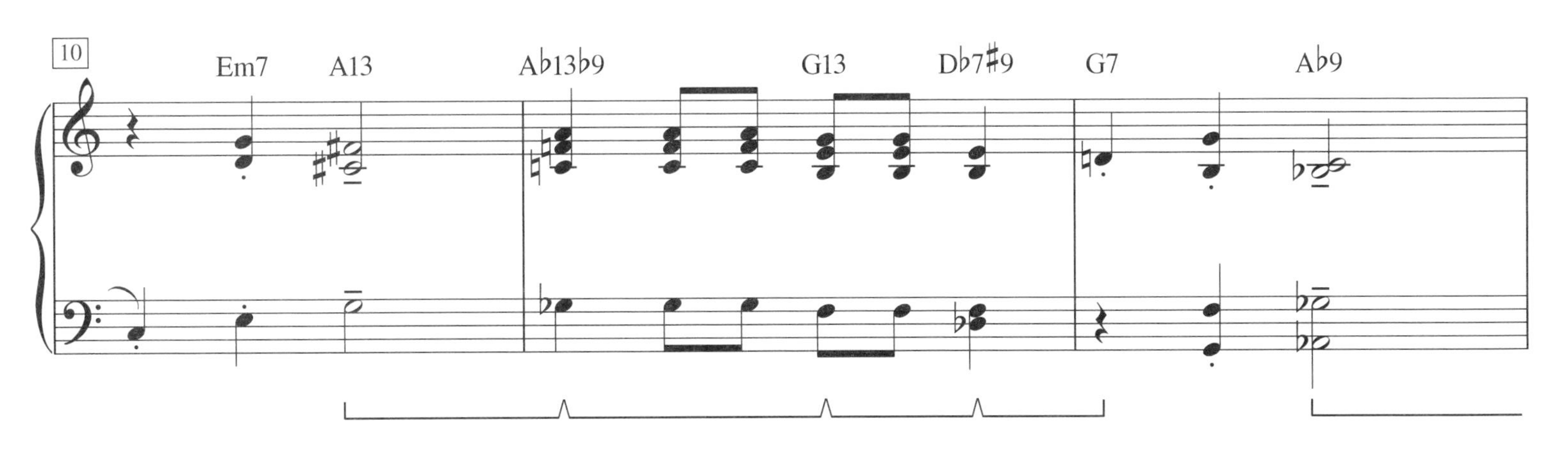

13
F6
Em7
A7♭9
f
16
Dm7
G7♭9
N.C.
G13♯11
C
p
f
p
19
G♭maj7♯5 A♭maj7♯5
N.C.
B♭13
A7
D7
G7
f
mf
22
C6
F13
C6
A♭9
G9
f
25
C7
B♭7♯9
A7♭9
A♭9
p
mf

28
F6 E♭7 Dm7 G13 C9
31
D♭9 C9 F13 C6/9 D9 G7 C6
34
F6 Em7 A7♭9 Dm7 G7♭9
f
p
37
N.C. G13♯11 C G♭maj7♯5 A♭maj7♯5 N.C.
f
p
f
mf
40
B♭13 A7 D7 G7 D♭9 C9
8va
p
f
p
8vb

THE PHILLIP KEVEREN SERIES

PIANO SOLO

Item	Title	Price
00156644	ABBA for Classical Piano	$15.99
00311024	Above All	$12.99
00311348	Americana	$12.99
00198473	Bach Meets Jazz	$14.99
00313594	Bacharach and David	$15.99
00306412	The Beatles	$19.99
00312189	The Beatles for Classical Piano	$17.99
00275876	The Beatles – Recital Suites	$19.99
00312546	Best Piano Solos	$15.99
00156601	Blessings	$14.99
00198656	Blues Classics	$14.99
00284359	Broadway Songs with a Classical Flair	$14.99
00310669	Broadway's Best	$16.99
00312106	Canzone Italiana	$12.99
00280848	Carpenters	$17.99
00310629	A Celtic Christmas	$14.99
00310549	The Celtic Collection	$14.99
00280571	Celtic Songs with a Classical Flair	$12.99
00263362	Charlie Brown Favorites	$14.99
00312190	Christmas at the Movies	$15.99
00294754	Christmas Carols with a Classical Flair	$12.99
00311414	Christmas Medleys	$14.99
00236669	Christmas Praise Hymns	$12.99
00233788	Christmas Songs for Classical Piano	$14.99
00311769	Christmas Worship Medleys	$14.99
00310607	Cinema Classics	$15.99
00301857	Circles	$10.99
00311101	Classic Wedding Songs	$12.99
00311292	Classical Folk	$10.95
00311083	Classical Jazz	$14.99
00137779	Coldplay for Classical Piano	$16.99
00311103	Contemporary Wedding Songs	$12.99
00348788	Country Songs with a Classical Flair	$14.99
00249097	Disney Recital Suites	$17.99
00311754	Disney Songs for Classical Piano	$17.99
00241379	Disney Songs for Ragtime Piano	$17.99
00364812	The Essential Hymn Anthology	$34.99
00311881	Favorite Wedding Songs	$14.99
00315974	Fiddlin' at the Piano	$12.99
00311811	The Film Score Collection	$15.99
00269408	Folksongs with a Classical Flair	$12.99
00144353	The Gershwin Collection	$14.99
00233789	Golden Scores	$14.99
00144351	Gospel Greats	$14.99
00183566	The Great American Songbook	$14.99
00312084	The Great Melodies	$14.99
00311157	Great Standards	$14.99
00171621	A Grown-Up Christmas List	$14.99
00311071	The Hymn Collection	$14.99
00311349	Hymn Medleys	$14.99
00280705	Hymns in a Celtic Style	$14.99
00269407	Hymns with a Classical Flair	$14.99
00311249	Hymns with a Touch of Jazz	$14.99
00310905	I Could Sing of Your Love Forever	$16.99
00310762	Jingle Jazz	$15.99
00175310	Billy Joel for Classical Piano	$16.99
00126449	Elton John for Classical Piano	$19.99
00310839	Let Freedom Ring!	$12.99
00238988	Andrew Lloyd Webber Piano Songbook	$14.99
00313227	Andrew Lloyd Webber Solos	$17.99
00313523	Mancini Magic	$16.99
00312113	More Disney Songs for Classical Piano	$16.99
00311295	Motown Hits	$14.99
00300640	Piano Calm	$12.99
00339131	Piano Calm: Christmas	$14.99
00346009	Piano Calm: Prayer	$14.99
00306870	Piazzolla Tangos	$17.99
00386709	Praise and Worship for Classical Piano	$14.99
00156645	Queen for Classical Piano	$17.99
00310755	Richard Rodgers Classics	$17.99
00289545	Scottish Songs	$12.99
00119403	The Sound of Music	$16.99
00311978	The Spirituals Collection	$12.99
00366023	So Far...	$14.99
00210445	Star Wars	$16.99
00224738	Symphonic Hymns for Piano	$14.99
00366022	Three-Minute Encores	$16.99
00279673	Tin Pan Alley	$12.99
00312112	Treasured Hymns for Classical Piano	$15.99
00144926	The Twelve Keys of Christmas	$14.99
00278486	The Who for Classical Piano	$16.99
00294036	Worship with a Touch of Jazz	$14.99
00311911	Yuletide Jazz	$19.99

EASY PIANO

Item	Title	Price
00210401	Adele for Easy Classical Piano	$17.99
00310610	African-American Spirituals	$12.99
00218244	The Beatles for Easy Classical Piano	$14.99
00218387	Catchy Songs for Piano	$12.99
00310973	Celtic Dreams	$12.99
00233686	Christmas Carols for Easy Classical Piano	$14.99
00311126	Christmas Pops	$16.99
00368199	Christmas Reflections	$14.99
00311548	Classic Pop/Rock Hits	$14.99
00310769	A Classical Christmas	$14.99
00310975	Classical Movie Themes	$12.99
00144352	Disney Songs for Easy Classical Piano	$14.99
00311093	Early Rock 'n' Roll	$14.99
00311997	Easy Worship Medleys	$14.99
00289547	Duke Ellington	$14.99
00160297	Folksongs for Easy Classical Piano	$12.99
00110374	George Gershwin Classics	$14.99
00310805	Gospel Treasures	$14.99
00306821	Vince Guaraldi Collection	$19.99
00160294	Hymns for Easy Classical Piano	$14.99
00310798	Immortal Hymns	$12.99
00311294	Jazz Standards	$12.99
00355474	Living Hope	$14.99
00310744	Love Songs	$14.99
00233740	The Most Beautiful Songs for Easy Classical Piano	$12.99
00220036	Pop Ballads	$14.99
00311406	Pop Gems of the 1950s	$12.95
00233739	Pop Standards for Easy Classical Piano	$12.99
00102887	A Ragtime Christmas	$12.99
00311293	Ragtime Classics	$14.99
00312028	Santa Swings	$14.99
00233688	Songs from Childhood for Easy Classical Piano	$12.99
00103258	Songs of Inspiration	$14.99
00310840	Sweet Land of Liberty	$12.99
00126450	10,000 Reasons	$16.99
00310712	Timeless Praise	$14.99
00311086	TV Themes	$14.99
00310717	21 Great Classics	$14.99
00160076	Waltzes & Polkas for Easy Classical Piano	$12.99
00145342	Weekly Worship	$17.99

BIG-NOTE PIANO

Item	Title	Price
00310838	Children's Favorite Movie Songs	$14.99
00346000	Christmas Movie Magic	$12.99
00277368	Classical Favorites	$12.99
00277370	Disney Favorites	$14.99
00310888	Joy to the World	$12.99
00310908	The Nutcracker	$12.99
00277371	Star Wars	$16.99

BEGINNING PIANO SOLOS

Item	Title	Price
00311202	Awesome God	$14.99
00310837	Christian Children's Favorites	$14.99
00311117	Christmas Traditions	$10.99
00311250	Easy Hymns	$12.99
00102710	Everlasting God	$10.99
00311403	Jazzy Tunes	$10.95
00310822	Kids' Favorites	$12.99
00367778	A Magical Christmas	$14.99
00338175	Silly Songs for Kids	$9.99

PIANO DUET

Item	Title	Price
00126452	The Christmas Variations	$14.99
00362562	Classic Piano Duets	$14.99
00311350	Classical Theme Duets	$12.99
00295099	Gospel Duets	$12.99
00311544	Hymn Duets	$14.99
00311203	Praise & Worship Duets	$14.99
00294755	Sacred Christmas Duets	$14.99
00119405	Star Wars	$16.99
00253545	Worship Songs for Two	$12.99

Prices, contents, and availability subject to change without notice.

HAL•LEONARD®

Search songlists, more products and place your order from your favorite music retailer at **halleonard.com**